50 STATES

500 PLACES TO VISIT

pil

Publications International, Ltd.

Contributing writers: Eric Peterson, David Lewis, Laura Sutherland, Melissa Arnold, Clark Norton, Christina Tree, and Jim Yenckel

Images: iStockphoto, Library of Congress, National Park Service, Shutterstock.com, and Wikimedia Commons

Louis Weber, CEO
Publications International, Ltd.
8140 Lehigh Avenue
Morton Grove, IL 60053

Permission is never granted for commercial purposes.

ISBN: 978-1-64030-455-0

Manufactured in China.

8 7 6 5 4 3 2 1

TABLE OF CONTENTS

MAINE

WHAT TO SEE AT ACADIA
Cadillac Mountain, Mount Desert, Islesford Historical Museum, Wild Gardens of Acadia

WHAT TO DO AT ACADIA
Hiking, fishing, climbing, bird-watching, swimming, boating, horseback riding, carriage-riding, bicycling, leaf peeping

The spectacular scenery that is **Acadia National Park** includes 26 mountains. Its rugged terrain and dramatic coastline make for some memorable sights.

ACADIA NATIONAL PARK

Situated off the coast of Maine, Acadia National Park covers nearly half of Mount Desert Island. Originally named Isles des Monts Deserts by explorer Samuel de Champlain in 1604, the island also boasts the towns of Bar Harbor, Southwest Harbor, Mount Desert, and Tremont.

From the coastline, you can see the island's barren mountaintops, sheared off by ancient glaciers. Cadillac Mountain, a granite-topped peak rising 1,532 feet, is the highest mountain along the north Atlantic seaboard.

Bass Harbor Head Light, built in 1858, marks the entrance to Bass Harbor on the southwest side of Mount Desert Island.

Jordan Pond is one of Acadia's many features formed by glaciers. The pond is bordered by Penobscot Mountain on the west and by two mountains known as "The Bubbles" to the northeast.

MAINE CITIES TO SEE

- Portland
- Lewiston
- Auburn
- Bangor
- Augusta
- Brunswick
- South Portland
- Biddeford
- Sanford
- Ogunquit

BOOTHBAY HARBOR

Boothbay Harbor, which lies along Maine's mid-coast, is a great place for watching whales and puffins, canoeing, kayaking, hiking, biking, mackerel fishing, and camping. The picturesque harbor is exactly how many people envision the state: Fishers haul in lobster traps, and masts gently rock in the distance. You can cruise to Monhegan Island or see sites such as the Maine Resources Aquarium; the Maine Maritime Museum; or Burnt Island Light, a lighthouse built in 1821.

(Left) The rugged **Boothbay Harbor** area is one of Maine's most beautiful destinations. You can rent cove-side cottages, dine in fine restaurants, and browse quaint waterfront shops.

Penobscot Bay is perfect for those who want to explore the real outdoors. Choose among recreational sports such as sailing, fishing, or hunting. The nearby towns of Camden, Bar Harbor, and Castine provide for more relaxing pursuits.

Explore the wild landscape of **Katahdin Woods and Waters National Monument** in northern Maine. This new national monument offers spectacular views of Mount Katahdin.

The **Old Port district** of Portland, Maine, is known for its cobblestone streets, old brick buildings, fishing piers, boutiques, shops, restaurants, cafés, and bars. The district is popular with tourists and locals alike.

NEW HAMPSHIRE

WHITE MOUNTAIN NATIONAL FOREST

New Hampshire's White Mountain National Forest is the heart of the White Mountains. Mount Washington rises fiercely above the dense woodlands to 6,288 feet, which makes it the highest mountain in the northeastern United States. On a clear day, you can see into New Hampshire, Maine, Vermont, Massachusetts, and Canada from its peak.

The vast majority of White Mountain National Forest's 800,000 acres are in New Hampshire, with the eastern edge creeping into Maine. The forest is indisputably nature's domain. It may be an easy drive from urban America, but it seems to be a million miles away.

(Above) The **Mount Washington Cog Railway**, completed in 1869, carries tourists up Mount Washington in New Hampshire.

(Below) An east–west shortcut through the heart of White Mountain National Forest, **Kancamagus Scenic Byway** accesses otherwise remote waterfalls, swimming holes, hiking trails, and campgrounds.

LAKE WINNIPESAUKEE

At 26 miles long and 15 miles across at its widest point, Lake Winnipesaukee is New Hampshire's largest lake. This glacial phenomenon has been a summer vacation hot spot for more than a century, attracting visitors from all over New England, including Boston, which is just a two-hour drive away. At Lake Winnipesaukee, you can hike, snowshoe, fish, and scuba dive.

(Right) Dozens of islands and the surrounding Ossipee and Sandwich mountain ranges add to **Lake Winnipesaukee**'s scenic splendor.

ODIORNE POINT STATE PARK

This state park includes Odiorne Point, the largest undeveloped stretch of shore on New Hampshire's 18-mile coast. Its spectacular oceanfront is backed by marshes, sand dunes, and dense vegetation. An extensive network of trails, including a paved bike path, winds through the park. There are also picnic areas, a boat launch, and a playground.

Kids will love visiting Odiorne's Seacoast Science Center to learn about the many creatures they're likely to spot in the tide pools. All kinds of sea urchins, starfish, mollusks, and crabs inhabit the shoreline's intertidal zone, and when the tide is low, there are many opportunities to see them.

(Left) **Odiorne Point State Park**, in Rye, New Hampshire, offers scenic views of the ocean and rocky shore.

Canterbury Shaker Village in Canterbury, New Hampshire, contains a museum, 25 original Shaker buildings, and 694 acres of fields, gardens, forests, and millponds. It was designated as a National Historic Landmark in 1993.

The Cornish–Windsor Bridge stretches 449 feet and 5 inches across the Connecticut River, linking Cornish, New Hampshire, with Windsor, Vermont. It was the longest covered bridge still standing in the U.S. until 2008.

Visit the **Flume Gorge** in Franconia Notch State Park, New Hampshire. The natural gorge extends 800 feet at the base of Mount Liberty.

VERMONT

GREEN MOUNTAINS

The Green Mountains of Vermont are full of surprises. The historic range is a great place for caving, hiking, skiing, and gawking at the splendid natural beauty. The 250-mile-long Green Mountains become the Berkshires to the south, in Massachusetts; to the west is Lake Champlain; and to the east are the White Mountains of New Hampshire. The 385,000-acre Green Mountain National Forest is the public's entry to the mountains. The national forest was formed in 1932 after floods and fires exacerbated by excessive logging threatened the region.

Sailing is one way to enjoy the pristine waters of **Lake Champlain**.

LAKE CHAMPLAIN

Samuel de Champlain explored so much of New England that it was only fair to name the spectacular Lake Champlain after him. He discovered the lake in 1609 while in the Champlain Valley, which lies between Vermont's Green Mountains and the Adirondack Mountains of New York. Lake Champlain has since served the needs of merchants and mariners, scalawags and soldiers, smugglers and spies, and patriots and traitors. The lake has seen its share of naval conflict, too. In 1814, troops led by U.S. Commodore Thomas McDonough defeated the British Navy in a fierce fight. During the 19th century, canal boats and steamboats carried coal, timber, iron ore, and grain across the lake. Today, industry has given way to recreation.

Lake Champlain has become a year-round playground featuring boating, hiking, skiing, snowshoeing, snowmobiling, ice climbing, and rock climbing. Bicyclists take advantage of the Lake Champlain Bikeways' 35 loops and 10- to 60-mile tours.

Historic family farms are sprinkled within the dense forest that sheaths the **Green Mountains.**

THE VERMONT INSTITUTE OF NATURAL SCIENCE

The Vermont Institute of Natural Science (VINS) Nature Center in Quechee is the leading New England care center for injured raptors—owls, falcons, hawks, eagles, and vultures, about 25 species in all—that can no longer survive in the wild. The center receives birds from all over the United States and houses them in specially adapted high-ceilinged cages. Guests can enjoy bird-watching along the center's picturesque nature trails.

Bald eagles are among the birds of prey cared for at the **VINS Nature Center.**

BEN & JERRY'S ICE CREAM FACTORY

Vermont's top tourist attraction is Ben & Jerry's Ice Cream Factory in Waterbury. Ben Cohen and Jerry Greenfield began making their ice cream in the neighborhood in 1978; today, they sell their products all over the world. All around the brightly painted factory grounds are unusual items for kids to climb on, as well as a small playground and picnic tables.

The tour at the **Ben & Jerry's Ice Cream Factory** offers a glimpse of the ice cream-making process. Be sure to visit the Flavor Graveyard, where colorful tombstones honor dearly departed flavors.

Shelburne Farms is a nonprofit education center, working farm, and National Historic Landmark in Shelburne, Vermont. Visitors can enjoy the walking trails, children's farmyard, inn, restaurant, property tours, and special events.

Vermont has some of the largest ski areas in New England. The **Killington Resort** in Killington, Vermont, includes 1,509 skiable acres, 155 trails, and 21 lifts.

The Vermont State House in Montpelier is the state's capitol and seat of the Vermont General Assembly. The building, which was designated a National Historic Landmark in 1970, is open to visitors with few restrictions whether or not the legislature is in session.

RHODE ISLAND

Amble along the famous **Cliff Walk** in Newport, Rhode Island. You can pick up the trail along Newport's eastern shore, and you'll eventually end up at Easton's Beach.

BENEFIT STREET

If you're touring Providence, Rhode Island, and its antique treasures, the best place to start is Benefit Street, also known as the "Mile of History." Benefit Street was established in 1756 and became home to Providence's well-to-do merchants. Today, almost all the buildings along the "Mile of History" have been restored, giving the street the architectural flavor of colonial times. While many of the building interiors are off-limits to the public, visitors can take in the historical ambience of this collection of homes and businesses.

(Right) Just around the corner from Benefit Street is the **John Brown House Museum**. Providence's John Brown was a politician who completed the mansion in 1788. John Quincy Adams proclaimed the house "the most magnificent and elegant private mansion that I have ever seen on this continent."

Among the most elaborate of Newport's exquisite mansions is **The Breakers**, Cornelius Vanderbilt II's summer home. It was named for the waves that crash into the rocks below the estate.

NEWPORT MANSIONS

Newport is a small city on Aquidneck Island, Rhode Island, in Narragansett Bay. Visitors can explore Newport's spectacular collection of mansions where America's wealthiest families, including the Vanderbilts, Astors, and Dukes, spent leisurely summers. Be sure to see The Breakers, Chateau-sur-Mer, Marble House, Hunter House, the Elms, and Rosecliff.

BLOCK ISLAND

Block Island is a tear-shape isle only three miles wide and seven miles long. The island lies 12 miles off the coast of Rhode Island and about 18 miles northeast of Long Island, New York. Block Island's beaches, windswept dunes, gently rolling hills, sandy cliffs, verdant valleys, and freshwater ponds have lured visitors for decades.

Lions, tigers, and bears—and just about every other animal you can imagine—are on display at the **Green Animals Topiary Garden** in Portsmouth, Rhode Island. Eighty topiary displays are available for public viewing.

Block Island Southeast Light, located on the island's Mohegan bluffs, was designated a National Historic Landmark in 1997. There is a small museum and gift shop in the lighthouse and the tower is open for tours in the summer.

Beavertail State Park, located at the southern end of Conanicut Island in Narragansett Bay, Rhode Island, offers some of the most beautiful vistas along the New England coastline. The park's main attraction is the Beavertail Lighthouse.

CONNECTICUT

The *Charles W. Morgan* is a whaling ship built in 1841. **Mystic Seaport** acquired the ship in 1941. The ship is among the collection of antique vessels anchored at Mystic Seaport.

MYSTIC SEAPORT

Mystic Seaport is one of the nation's leading maritime museums. It was founded in 1929 to preserve seagoing culture. The museum's grounds cover 19 acres in Mystic, Connecticut, and include a recreated New England coastal village, a working shipyard, and artifact storage facilities.

Mystic Seaport expanded in the 1940s. Historic buildings—including the Buckingham-Hall House (a coastal farmhouse), the Nautical Instruments Shop, the Mystic Press Printing Office, and the Boardman School one-room schoolhouse—were moved from their original locations in New England and put together to form Mystic Seaport, a model New England seagoing village. Mystic Seaport became one of the first living museums.

Mystic Seaport has assembled one of the largest collections of maritime history. The collections include marine paintings, scrimshaw, models, tools, ships plans, film and video recordings, and more than one million photographs. These collections are on display at Mystic Seaport's Collections Research Center storage and preservation facility.

STONINGTON BOROUGH

The town of Stonington is the oldest borough in Connecticut (Stonington Borough), settled in 1753 and chartered in 1801. Both the lighthouse and the town represent the history and architecture of an archetypal Connecticut town. The Old Lighthouse Museum is in the restored 30-foot granite tower. The current lighthouse (completed in 1840) was built with salvaged materials from the original lighthouse (built in 1823). The museum's exhibits illustrate the history of this coastal region, which is notable for its beautiful Stonington stoneware.

The Stonington Historical Society acquired the lighthouse in 1925 and opened it as a museum in 1927. The **Old Lighthouse Museum** honors the maritime history of this quaint coastal village.

Explore a former residence of American actor William Gillette at **Gillette Castle State Park** in East Haddam. Since the state of Connecticut bought the property in 1943, visitors have gawked at the castle's stone exterior and admired its interior woodwork.

CONNECTICUT PLACES TO VISIT

- Yale Peabody Museum of Natural History (New Haven)
- Mystic Aquarium (Mystic)
- Mashantucket Pequot Museum & Research Center (Mashantucket)
- Lake Compounce amusement park (Bristol)
- Dinosaur State Park (Rocky Hill)
- New England Air Museum (Windsor Locks)
- Aldrich Contemporary Art Museum (Ridgefield)
- Roseland Cottage (Woodstock)
- Cove Island Park (Stamford)

Weir Farm National Historic Site includes historic homes and art studios used by American Impressionist J. Alden Weir and sculptor Mahonri Young. Weir Farm is located in both Ridgefield and Wilton, Connecticut.

MASSACHUSETTS

FREEDOM TRAIL

Follow the red brick line along the 2.5-mile Freedom Trail in Boston and take in 300 years of American history. The 16 sites along the trail describe the city's early patriots, their notion of liberty, and the journey to independence.

The idea for the Freedom Trail came in 1958 from William Schofield, an editorial writer for the *Boston Herald-Traveler*. He hatched the idea of creating a marked line that would transform Boston's mazelike streets into something tourists could follow. His campaign succeeded and inspired other "trails," including Boston's Black Heritage Trail.

The tour officially begins at the 50-acre Boston Common, which was a British troop encampment during the American Revolution. Other sites along the trail include the Massachusetts State House, Park Street Church, Old South Meeting House, Paul Revere House, and Bunker Hill Monument.

The **Old State House** is a stop on the Freedom Trail and the site of the Boston Massacre. Built in 1713, the Old State House was at the center of civic events that sparked the American Revolution. It now serves as a history museum.

A tour of **Fenway Park** is a must for any fan of America's favorite pastime.

FENWAY PARK

Fenway Park reigns as a temple of baseball, despite the decades of misfortune for its principal occupant, the Boston Red Sox. Built in 1912, Fenway is Major League Baseball's oldest park. The stadium's seating capacity is under 38,000 people, and while the team suffered an 86-year dry spell beginning in 1918, Red Sox fans continued to crowd Fenway. Fans were finally rewarded in 2004 (and again in 2007 and 2013) when Boston won the World Series. Fenway's atmosphere is magical and not-to-be missed when in Boston.

BOSTON'S PUBLIC GARDEN

A 24-acre garden within a city, Boston's Public Garden has been a favorite among tourists for years. The beautifully landscaped area gives sightseers the chance to rest their tired feet.

The famous swan boats at **Boston's Public Garden** are especially popular during the spring and summer months.

MORE BOSTON ATTRACTIONS

- Boston Children's Museum
- Museum of Fine Arts
- Boston Harbor Islands
- New England Holocaust Memorial
- John F. Kennedy Presidential Library and Museum
- Boston Tea Party Ships and Museum
- Isabella Stewart Gardner Museum
- The Mapparium

OLD STURBRIDGE VILLAGE

Families who want to experience life in times past will be enthralled by Old Sturbridge Village, just an hour's drive west of Boston. The largest outdoor living history museum in the northeast, Old Sturbridge Village brings to life an 1830s New England rural community, down to the smallest details.

Costumed interpreters demonstrate daily tasks of farmers, blacksmiths, shoemakers, tinsmiths, housewives, and crafts-people at **Old Sturbridge Village**.

HARVARD SQUARE

Harvard Square in Cambridge, Massachusetts, is a great place to go if you want to feel young, hip, and smart. Teeming with Harvard professors, students, and wannabes, "the Square" can give visitors the sense that they are attending Harvard without having to take exams.

Harvard Square is packed with cafés, shops, and bookstores. A number of Harvard museums are within walking distance of the Square.

SALEM

Salem, Massachusetts, calls itself "Witch City" and is so named for that harrowing seven-month period in 1692 when the townspeople put 19 innocent people to death. Today, Salem offers numerous places devoted to witches and their kind.

The **Salem Witch Museum** brings visitors back to early Salem through a dramatic presentation that uses stage sets with life-size figures, lighting, and narration. It also gives visitors an excellent overview of the Salem Witch Trials.

PLYMOUTH ROCK

People flock to Plymouth, Massachusetts, to watch whales, relax on the beach, kayak, and see the famous ten-ton granite boulder, Plymouth Rock. Plymouth Rock is hallowed in American history as the place where the Pilgrims set foot in America. They went on to form the first permanent European settlement in New England. While the first mention of the site came nearly a century after the *Mayflower* landed, this is the accepted spot where Pilgrims landed and started Plymouth Colony.

Martha's Vineyard, an island off the coast of Massachusetts, provides an old-fashioned beach vacation with pristine beaches, clean salty air, lavish beachfront homes, and rolling farmlands. Its picturesque towns are filled with ice cream shops, sea captains' stately houses, and art galleries.

Plymouth Rock marks the site where the Pilgrims were thought to have landed in 1620. Today you can see Plymouth Rock at Pilgrim Memorial State Park.

Walden Pond in Concord, Massachusetts, inspired author Henry David Thoreau's most famous work, *Walden,* which is often credited with creating the conservation movement.

WALDEN POND

Henry David Thoreau moved to Walden Pond in Concord, Massachusetts, to get a little peace and quiet and to write. He wrote an account of his time there called *Walden; or, Life in the Woods.* In Thoreau's day, the land around the pond was one of the few woods left in the area. Today, Walden Pond is part of Massachusetts's Walden Pond State Reservation, which includes the 61-acre pond plus another 2,680 acres known as "Walden Woods."

NEW YORK

STATUE OF LIBERTY

The Statue of Liberty is one of the must-see sites for any tourist in New York City. Every year, about 4 million people visit the monument, which proudly stands on Liberty Island in New York Harbor. Lady Liberty stands more than 151 feet high but reaches greater heights thanks to the 65-foot-high foundation and the 89-foot-high granite pedestal. The statue is a massive iron pylon with a skeletal structure (engineered by Gustav Eiffel of Eiffel Tower fame) clad with copper skin sculpted by Frederic Auguste Bartholdi.

ELLIS ISLAND

The Statue of Liberty National Monument includes Liberty Island, site of the Statue of Liberty, and Ellis Island. Between 1892 and 1954, Ellis Island served as the immigration station for more than 12 million people who came to make America their home. Today, the site is a museum.

The **Ellis Island National Museum of Immigration** has three floors of exhibits documenting immigrants' experiences at Ellis Island, as well as the general history of immigration to the United States.

"Liberty Enlightening the World" is a tourist attraction, a symbol, an icon, and a monument to Franco-American relations.

Foundation Hall in the museum contains the Last Column. This beam from the South Tower was removed in 2002, closing out the recovery period. During that recovery period, workers left tributes and photographs on the column, which are preserved at the museum.

NATIONAL SEPTEMBER 11 MEMORIAL & MUSEUM

The deadly terrorist attacks on September 11, 2001, killed thousands, shocked the nation, and left the city of New York altered forever. Where the Twin Towers of the World Trade Center once stood, there are now two massive reflecting pools, part of the National September 11 Memorial & Museum. Great waterfalls pour into the pools, with the victims' names inscribed around them. The Memorial Plaza opened in September 2011, ten years after the attacks. The museum, which opened a few years later in 2014, includes physical artifacts from the tragedy, audio and video recordings, and photographs of the victims.

CENTRAL PARK

Central Park is the recreational center of life in Manhattan, New York City. Frederick Law Olmsted and Calvert Vaux designed the park after winning an 1858 design competition. Today, Central Park hosts activities from alfresco dining while listening to the Metropolitan Opera to strolling through formal gardens or exploring the zoo. In the summer, the Public Theater presents a Shakespeare in the Park series. Be sure to see the Bethesda Fountain, the Carousel, the Strawberry Fields memorial to John Lennon, and the Conservatory Garden.

America's first landscaped public park covers 843 acres and is 2.5 miles long and half a mile wide. **Central Park** has a 6.1-mile loop for cars that has parallel paths for horses, joggers, and cyclists during the week, but the park is closed to motorists on weekends.

HIGH LINE

The High Line is a 1.45-mile-long elevated linear park. It was created on a former New York Central Railroad line on the west side of Manhattan in New York City.

(Right) Since opening in 2009, the **High Line** has become an icon in contemporary landscape architecture, urban design, and ecology.

TIMES SQUARE

New York City's Times Square is a blaring, electrifying, exhilarating, intoxicating, spotlit "crossroads of the world." Times Square welcomes more than 30 million visitors annually to its stores, hotels, restaurants, theaters, and attractions. The first electric billboard went up in 1917, and Times Square has been synonymous with glitz ever since. While as crowded and crazy as ever, Times Square today is also tourist- and family-friendly.

(Left) Dazzling neon signs and advertisements have made **Times Square** a New York City icon.

ROCKEFELLER CENTER

Midtown Manhattan's Rockefeller Center is a complex of 19 commercial buildings a few blocks south of Central Park. The center is a shopping mall, an art deco icon, and a winter wonderland. The center of the complex is 30 Rockefeller Plaza, a 70-story building that towers above the skating rink and the adjacent central plaza. Visitors can enjoy dancing accompanied by a big band in the Rainbow Room or stop by Radio City Music Hall, one of the largest indoor theaters in the United States, where the Rockettes have been knocking out audiences since 1932.

Rockefeller Center is the only place on Earth where you can nurse a cocktail and watch ice-skaters twirl beneath a big, golden statue of Prometheus.

On a clear day, you can see 80 miles from the observation deck of the **Empire State Building**. The building overlooks such landmarks as Rockefeller Center, the United Nations, Central Park, the Statue of Liberty, and the Chrysler Building, which is another art deco building.

BROOKLYN BRIDGE

The Brooklyn Bridge opened on May 24, 1883, linking what would become the boroughs of Brooklyn and Manhattan in New York City. It was an engineering accomplishment of mythic proportions. In its day, the Brooklyn Bridge was the longest suspension bridge in the world, with the length of the main span measuring 1,595 feet.

The **Brooklyn Bridge**, designed by architect John Augustus Roebling, towers over New York City's East River.

SOLOMON R. GUGGENHEIM MUSEUM

Viewed from Fifth Avenue, the exterior of the Solomon R. Guggenheim Museum is an inverted cone with wide bands rising upward. Inside, the museum contains an atrium and a spiral ramp where visitors view artwork from a perspective that can be dizzying. The museum has works by Kandinsky, Klee, Calder, Picasso, Rousseau, and many more.

The **Guggenheim Museum** in New York City is known for both its collections and its adventurous architecture.

MUST-SEE NYC MUSEUMS

- Metropolitan Museum of Art
- Solomon R. Guggenheim Museum
- Museum of Modern Art
- Ellis Island National Museum of Immigration
- Lower East Side Tenement Museum
- Whitney Museum of American Art

COOPERSTOWN

Visitors to Cooperstown, New York, enjoy the Farmers' Museum, the Fenimore Art Museum, and the National Baseball Hall of Fame. The National Baseball Hall of Fame is by far the biggest draw. More people visit the National Baseball Hall of Fame every day than actually live in Cooperstown. The museum of baseball memorabilia is packed with rare old photographs, displays, and timelines that trace the history of the game and showcase its most important players, stadiums, and leagues. You'll see Babe Ruth's record-making bat, Willie Mays's glove, and Lou Gehrig's locker.

The hall showcases the plaques of the revered first five inductees: Ty Cobb, Babe Ruth, Honus Wagner, Christy Mathewson, and Walter Johnson.

PLACES TO VISIT IN NEW YORK STATE

- Niagara Falls State Park (Niagara Falls)
- Saratoga National Historical Park (Stillwater)
- Fire Island National Seashore (Fire Island)
- Erie Canalway (Upstate New York)
- Hudson River Valley (Albany)
- Harriet Tubman National Historical Park (Auburn)
- Home of Franklin D. Roosevelt (Hyde Park)
- Women's Rights National Historical Park (Seneca Falls)
- African Burial Ground National Monument (New York City)

NEW JERSEY

ATLANTIC CITY BOARDWALK

Just off the mainland of southeastern New Jersey lies Absecon Island, whose marshes and sandy beaches lay undisturbed until 1854. Then the Camden and Atlantic Railroad Line was built there, and Atlantic City was born. Unfortunately, the hordes of vacationers dragged volumes of sand through too many marbled lobbies.

In 1870, Alexander Boardman, a railroad conductor, proposed constructing a wooden walkway to sift out the sand, thus creating the Atlantic City Boardwalk. It is more than 4 miles long and 60 feet wide and features steel pilings and 40-foot steel beams. The Boardwalk helped make Atlantic City an attractive host city. Casino gambling was legalized here in the late 1970s and today the Boardwalk is open 24 hours a day.

CAPE MAY

Cape May is a peninsula at the southernmost tip of New Jersey; it's also the nation's oldest seaside resort. Whalers settled Cape May in the 17th century, and today it's a magnet for visitors from New Jersey, New York, and eastern Pennsylvania.

Cape May is the gateway to the 30 miles of sandy Atlantic Ocean beaches along the Jersey Cape that connect the resort towns of Ocean City, Sea Isle City, Avalon, Stone Harbor, and the Wildwoods. You'll find plenty of attractions here, including picturesque gardens and Early-American museums. You can also charter fishing boats, rent speedboats, kayak, or parasail.

(Below) Because a fire swept **Cape May** in 1878, it was rebuilt in the Victorian style of the day, setting the architectural tone for what remains a charming, old-fashioned resort.

(Left) Boardwalk visitors enjoy a range of distractions, from saltwater taffy and chocolate fudge stands to the **Steel Pier**'s rides and games.

The **Cape May Lighthouse** towers 157 feet high and serves as a peaceful sentry over the picturesque peninsula.

NEW JERSEY PINE BARRENS

New Jersey Pinelands National Reserve, better known as the Pine Barrens, comprises impenetrable bogs and marshes with forests of low pine and oak, sporadic stands of cedar, and hardwood swamps. Tourists love hiking, biking, boating, picking cranberries, and visiting the historic villages of Batsto and Double Trouble.

The 1.1-million-acre **New Jersey Pinelands National Reserve** is about the size of Glacier National Park in Montana.

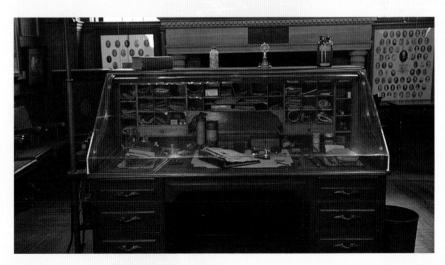

Visit the home and laboratory of America's greatest inventor at the **Thomas Edison National Historical Park** in West Orange, New Jersey.

DELAWARE

FIRST STATE NATIONAL HISTORICAL PARK

First State National Historical Park consists of seven different sites in Delaware: Beaver Valley, Fort Christina, Old Swedes Church, New Castle Court House, the Green (Dover), John Dickinson Plantation, and Ryves Holt House. The park covers the history of Colonial Delaware and the role it played leading up to American Independence. It also tells the story of early Dutch, Swedish, Finnish, and English settlers.

Fort Christina preserves the original site where Swedish and Finnish settlers landed in 1638 and built the colony of New Sweden. The park includes a reconstructed Swedish log cabin.

Visit **Winterthur**, the lavish former home of Henry Francis du Pont, to see its collection of American decorative arts and meander through its 60-acre garden. Families enjoy Enchanted Woods, the three-acre fairytale children's garden.

DELAWARE PLACES TO VISIT
- Hagley Museum and Library (Wilmington)
- Nemours Mansion and Gardens (Wilmington)
- Fort Delaware State Park (Pea Patch Island)
- Air Mobility Command Museum (Dover)
- Town of Rehoboth Beach

DUQUESNE INCLINE

One of the best ways to see Pittsburgh, Pennsylvania, is by taking the Duquesne Incline, which, since 1877, has provided public transportation to the top of Mount Washington, a steep hill on the city's south side. Take the incline at night and go to the observation deck overlooking downtown Pittsburgh's Golden Triangle. Fifteen major bridges span the waters of the Allegheny and Monongahela rivers as they flow together to become the Ohio River. You'll be rewarded by the view and will land in the middle of Pittsburgh's Restaurant Row.

Opposite Mount Washington, going north across the rivers, is the Andy Warhol Museum, the Carnegie Science Center, PNC Park, and Heinz Field. While you're on the north side of the rivers, check out the National Aviary. It's a warm refuge on a chilly Pittsburgh day.

PENNSYLVANIA

INDEPENDENCE NATIONAL HISTORICAL PARK

Independence Hall, which is part of a 45-acre park (along with 20 or so other buildings), is where America's independence was born. Once called the Pennsylvania State House, this simple building in Philadelphia's Center City saw the foundations of the Declaration of Independence laid and brought to fruition.

The comely two-story redbrick building now has a steeple with a clock in it. But long ago, that steeple housed the 2,080-pound Liberty Bell. It chimed often (supposedly annoying the neighbors), but most notably, it was rung on July 8, 1776, to announce the first public reading of the Declaration of Independence. Now the bell is perhaps best known for its cracks—and its silence. The bell no longer hangs in the Independence Hall steeple because it has its own home on the park grounds.

The Independence National Historical Park covers three large city blocks. Follow the paths (quaint alleys) to the many historical buildings and fascinating sites, such as Ben Franklin's final resting place in the Christ Church graveyard. It's hallowed ground you're walking on, so take your time, and try to see as much as you can. It's a visit you'll always remember.

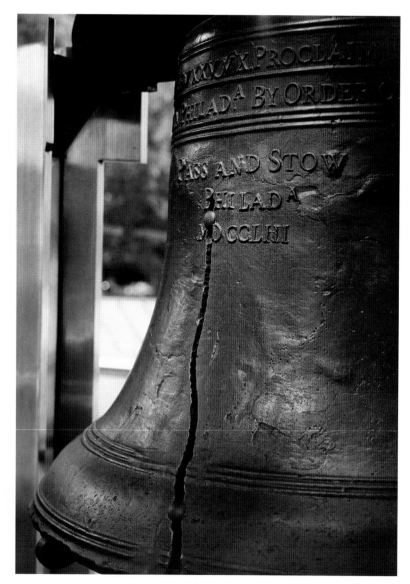

(Above) The **Liberty Bell** is now displayed in a glass chamber at the Liberty Bell Center.

(Left) Construction on the Pennsylvania State House, now called **Independence Hall**, began in 1732 and was completed 21 years later.

PHILADELPHIA'S OLD CITY

The heart of Philadelphia is its Old City neighborhood, where the metropolis began. And the heart of Old City is Elfreth's Alley, the oldest residential street in America, where people have lived since 1702. Three hundred years ago, traders and merchants lived in the Georgian- and Federal-style buildings on the narrow street. Blacksmith Jeremiah Elfreth owned most of the property along the alley and rented his houses to shipbuilders, sea captains, and landlubbers such as pewter smiths.

Today, Old City is a vibrant neighborhood that is filled with theater companies, art galleries, restaurants, shops, and bars. Christ Church, the Betsy Ross House, and Independence Hall are a short stroll away. Architecture fans should head to Elfreth's Alley Museum, which offers guided tours of homes that were built between 1710 and 1825.

Elfreth's Alley in Philadelphia is the oldest residential street in America.

The unique balconies of **Fallingwater** seem to float over the falls.

FALLINGWATER

Frank Lloyd Wright is probably the most famous American architect, and his most renowned building is a house in Mill Run, Pennsylvania, called Fallingwater. Wright designed the house in 1935 for Mr. and Mrs. Edgar J. Kaufmann of Pittsburgh. It was completed in 1939.

The location for the building was inspired by Edgar Kaufmann's love for the waterfall on Bear Run, the stream that runs through these serene woods. Wright also recognized the beauty of the location, and immediately visualized a house with cantilevered balconies on the rock bank over the waterfall.

Fallingwater became the gem of Wright's organic architecture school. A 1991 survey of the American Institute of Architects members judged it the all-time-best work of American architecture.

Today Fallingwater is open to the public and contains the original Wright-designed furnishings and the Kaufmanns' superb modern and Japanese art collections. There are the exterior views of the place, which suggest that art and nature are not so far apart.

GETTYSBURG

Gettysburg, Pennsylvania, was the site of one of the most pivotal battles of the Civil War. The clash during the first three days of July 1863 led to the eventual defeat of the Confederacy.

Gettysburg will forever be remembered as the place where General George Gordon Meade's Union forces turned back the Confederate Army of General Robert E. Lee, and as the location where President Abraham Lincoln gave his famous address four months later. Gettysburg offers visitors a surprising array of historic battlegrounds, monuments, and activities such as hiking and biking. Gettysburg includes the national park, the adjacent borough, and the next-door Eisenhower National Historic Site.

The Gettysburg area provides visitors with the opportunity to take a solemn pilgrimage to the hallowed site where 50,000 soldiers were killed, wounded, captured, or went missing in action during the Civil War. Gettysburg is also a charming tourist town with such attractions as the Gettysburg Heritage Center, the Jennie Wade House Museum, the Lincoln Train Museum, and the Gettysburg Battle Theater.

But the foundation of Gettysburg is really the 6,000-acre battlefield and its more than 1,400 markers and monuments. It is well worth the trip to see the now-peaceful hills and fields where the tide of the Civil War changed.

Gettysburg was the Civil War's bloodiest battle and was also the inspiration for President Abraham Lincoln's famous "Gettysburg Address."

Horse-drawn carriages are a common sight in **Pennsylvania Dutch Country** (Lancaster County). The area draws many visitors, curious to see a way of life that doesn't include modern conveniences.

PENNSYLVANIA PLACES TO VISIT

- Carnegie Science Center (Pittsburgh)
- Andy Warhol Museum (Pittsburgh)
- Gettysburg National Military Park (Gettysburg)
- Philadelphia Museum of Art (Philadelphia)
- Flight 93 National Memorial (Shanksville)
- Fort Necessity National Battlefield (Farmington)
- Frank Lloyd Wright's Fallingwater house (Mill Run)
- Hershey Park amusement park (Hershey)
- Valley Forge National Historical Park (Valley Forge)
- Pennsylvania State Capitol (Harrisburg)

MARYLAND

BALTIMORE INNER HARBOR

The showpiece of Baltimore, Maryland, is its fantastic Inner Harbor. Not long ago, the city's harbor could have served as urban decay's exhibit A. Then, beginning in the early 1960s, a succession of city administrations focused on rehabilitating the old waterfront. They succeeded beyond anyone's wildest dreams, luring many top-notch attractions. These include the National Aquarium, the Maryland Science Center, the Port Discovery Children's Museum, the Historic Ships in Baltimore Museum, the Civil War-era USS *Constellation*, and much more. Another must-see is the Top of the World Observation Level on the 27th floor of Baltimore's World Trade Center.

The **National Aquarium**, on the end of Baltimore's Pier 3, anchors the Baltimore Inner Harbor. The huge attraction has more than 10,500 fish and other creatures on display.

MARYLAND PLACES TO VISIT

- Oriole Park at Camden Yards (Baltimore)
- Fort McHenry National Monument (Baltimore)
- Harriet Tubman Underground Railroad National Historical Park (Cambridge)
- Assateague Island National Seashore (Assateague Island)
- Antietam National Battlefield (Sharpsburg)
- Catoctin Mountain Park (Thurmont)
- Oxon Cove Park (Oxon Hill)
- Glen Echo Park (Glen Echo)
- Greenbelt Park (Greenbelt)
- Brookside Gardens (Silver Spring)

ASSATEAGUE ISLAND

Off the coasts of Maryland and Virginia is an island with white sand beaches sparkling in the sunshine. Assateague Island is 37 miles long and is populated with wild horses that have galloped along the beach since the 1600s. Three stunning public parks share the island's 39,727 acres: Maryland's Assateague State Park, Assateague Island National Seashore, and Chincoteague National Wildlife Refuge.

Assateague Island's horses are descendants of domestic horses that reverted back to the wild. They are only about 12 to 13 hands tall—the size of ponies.

ANNAPOLIS

Annapolis, Maryland, is known as the sailing capital of America and home to the U.S. Naval Academy. Schooners, sailing sloops, and cruise boats offer a variety of trips, narrated tours, and even Sunday brunch. You can also take a guided kayak tour of downtown Annapolis or paddle alone on the many creeks that feed the bay.

Annapolis Harbor is a fascinating place for families to explore and is sure to spark the imagination of fledgling sailors.

WASHINGTON, D.C.

NATIONAL MALL

The National Mall in Washington, D.C., is one of the world's great public places. Its 146 acres of renowned monuments, impressive institutions, and grand government offices draw visitors from across the country and around the world.

By strict definition, "the Mall" means the greensward and adjacent buildings from the Washington Monument to the U.S. Capitol. But the broader area of the National Mall includes dozens of world-class museums, memorials, and other features worth exploring.

THE NATIONAL MALL AND SURROUNDING AREA INCLUDES:

- National Air and Space Museum
- World War II Memorial
- Constitution Gardens
- National Gallery of Art
- Martin Luther King Jr. Memorial
- National Museum of the American Indian
- Korean War and Vietnam Veterans memorials
- Franklin Delano Roosevelt Memorial
- Washington Monument
- Lincoln Memorial
- White House

The Smithsonian Institution offers eleven museums and galleries on the National Mall and six other museums and the National Zoo elsewhere in Washington, D.C. The Mall's Smithsonian Institution Building ("The Castle"), completed in 1855, serves as its visitor center.

U.S. CAPITOL

The U.S. Capitol is an icon of 19th-century neoclassical architecture that houses the country's legislative branches and stands as a symbol of the United States. The building's cornerstone was laid on September 18, 1793, and it's been burnt, rebuilt, expanded, and restored since then.

The **U.S. Capitol**'s cast-iron dome was designed by architect Thomas U. Walter and constructed from 1855 to 1866. The Statue of Freedom was placed atop the dome in 1863.

LINCOLN MEMORIAL

The Lincoln Memorial leads visitors to contemplate what Lincoln accomplished and what he stood for. No poet or biographer has expressed this as well as Lincoln himself in his addresses at his second inauguration and at Gettysburg. Both speeches are carved into the memorial's walls. The base of the Lincoln Memorial covers roughly the same area as a football field. The statue measures 19 feet wide by 19 feet tall—its size was sharply increased when sculptor Daniel Chester French realized it would be overwhelmed by the memorial building's size. The building has 36 Doric columns, one for each state during Lincoln's presidency.

The **Lincoln Memorial** has come to symbolize freedom, democracy, national unity, and social justice.

IN THIS TEMPLE
AS IN THE HEARTS OF THE PEOPLE
FOR WHOM HE SAVED THE UNION
THE MEMORY OF ABRAHAM LINCOLN
IS ENSHRINED FOREVER

FRANKLIN DELANO ROOSEVELT MEMORIAL

On the west side of the Tidal Basin, the Franklin Delano Roosevelt Memorial pays respect to the nation's 32nd president. Dedicated in 1997, the memorial consists of four outdoor "rooms," each depicting one of FDR's four terms in office, and iconic FDR quotes are carved into the granite walls. The memorial includes quiet areas bounded by shade trees, waterfalls, and pools. The FDR Memorial is not only about the man, but also the tumultuous times, most notably the Great Depression and World War II, through which he guided the nation.

(Left) Sculptures at the **Franklin Delano Roosevelt Memorial** such as this one were based on photographs of the 32nd president.

THOMAS JEFFERSON MEMORIAL

Located in East Potomac Park on the eastern shore of the Tidal Basin, the Thomas Jefferson Memorial, with its graceful dome, is a striking site. Known as a writer, philosopher, diplomat, and Renaissance man, the third president of the United States left behind a legacy of political ideas and actions that have passed the test of time. A statue of Jefferson stands at the center of the rotunda under the dome, and the surrounding walls are inscribed with words from his most lasting and eloquent writings, including personal letters and the Declaration of Independence.

The **Thomas Jefferson Memorial** was dedicated in 1943 on the 200th anniversary of Jefferson's birth.

The **National Cathedral** is the sixth-largest cathedral in the world.

NATIONAL CATHEDRAL

Pierre L'Enfant, Washington, D.C.'s first city planner, conceived of a national church in 1791. However, it took some time for L'Enfant's vision to come to pass. The foundation was laid in 1907, but the grand structure with more than 250 angels and more than 100 gargoyles was not finished for 83 years. The National Cathedral has been a focal point for spiritual life in the nation's capital since it opened in 1912. Every president has attended services here while in office. Many people have gathered at the church to mourn the passing of leaders or mark momentous events in world history.

ARLINGTON NATIONAL CEMETARY

Nearly four million visitors come to Arlington National Cemetery, across the Potomac from Washington, D.C., each year. Most come to pay respect to the leaders interred here or to thank the more than 300,000 people buried here, many of whom were soldiers killed in the line of duty. The original 200 acres were designated as a military cemetery on June 15, 1864. Soldiers and veterans from every war the United States has fought, from the Revolutionary War to the war in Iraq, are buried here (those who died prior to the Civil War were reinterred in Arlington after 1900).

The Tomb of the Unknowns contains the remains of service members from both World Wars and the conflict in Korea. (The Vietnam veteran who had been buried here was identified in 1998, and his body was returned to his family.) The Tomb is guarded 24 hours a day.

MORE D.C. ATTRACTIONS

- Fourth of July Fireworks
- National Cherry Blossom Festival
- United States Holocaust Memorial Museum
- National Museum of African American History and Culture
- Bureau of Engraving and Printing
- National Archives
- International Spy Museum
- West Potomac Park
- National Zoo
- Union Station

MONTICELLO

Monticello, the Virginia home of Thomas Jefferson, is a Roman neoclassical masterpiece. Jefferson moved onto the property in 1770, but the mansion was not completed until 1809, after Jefferson's second term as president. The house was the centerpiece of Jefferson's plantation. About 130 slaves worked the land, tended livestock, cooked, and cleaned there during Jefferson's life.

The west front of Jefferson's **Monticello** may seem familiar—it was exclusively featured on the back of the U.S. nickel from 1938 to 2003.

VIRGINIA

MOUNT VERNON ESTATE AND GARDENS

Mount Vernon was home to George Washington, the first president of the United States. The Virginia land was given to George Washington's great-grandfather in 1674, and it remained in the family for seven generations. Washington spent five years at Mount Vernon as a child and later lived there as an adult with his wife, Martha. The plantation grew to 8,000 acres while Washington served as commander in chief during the Revolutionary War. The estate is now 500 acres, 50 of which are open to the public.

Although Washington was best known as a military and political leader, he also designed and built many of the structures at **Mount Vernon**, including the famed mansion with its distinctive two-story portico.

COLONIAL WILLIAMSBURG

Williamsburg, Jamestown, and Yorktown make up Virginia's Historic Triangle. Known as Colonial Williamsburg, the area is the world's largest, and possibly greatest, living-history museum. Nowhere else is more care taken to create, recreate, and maintain a semblance of pre-Revolutionary life in the United States than here. Actors wear period clothing and interact with each other and the visiting public to simulate life in Williamsburg during the 17th century.

Today the **Colonial Williamsburg Fifes and Drums** are boys and girls ages 10 to 18 who carry on the tradition of military music.

VIRGINIA BEACH

Virginia Beach is a modern magnet for outdoors buffs—namely surfers, anglers, golfers, and boaters. The city is a favorite getaway with attractions ranging from amusement parks and miniature golf courses to historic sites and vibrant art. The beach is a wide, sandy strip on the central Atlantic coast, fronted by a three-mile boardwalk and oceanfront resorts with all the trimmings.

The original **Cape Henry Lighthouse** (built in 1792) at Fort Story in Virginia Beach was the first lighthouse structure authorized, completed, and lighted by the federal government. While the old lighthouse still stands, a new lighthouse was added in 1878.

Skyline Drive runs along the crest of the Blue Ridge, providing 75 overlooks and magnificent vistas of forests, mountains, and the Shenandoah Valley.

MORE VIRGINIA PLACES TO VISIT

- Natural Bridge Park (Rockbridge County)
- Steven F. Udvar-Hazy Center (Chantilly)
- Busch Gardens (Williamsburg)
- Appomattox Court House (Appomattox)
- Manassas National Battlefield Park (Manassas)
- Colonial National Historical Park (Jamestown, Yorktown)
- Chincoteague National Wildlife Refuge (Assateague Island)

SHENANDOAH VALLEY

Shenandoah Valley stretches from Harpers Ferry, West Virginia, to Roanoke and Salem, Virginia. Visit the valley in the spring or fall to see the fabulous blossoming flowers or autumn leaf displays. More than 500 miles of trails wind through the valley, including part of the Appalachian Trail.

WEST VIRGINIA

MONONGAHELA NATIONAL FOREST

The Monongahela National Forest in West Virginia is one of the largest tracts of protected Eastern woodlands. This makes it a hub for outdoorspeople of all stripes—anglers, hikers, mountain bikers, and paddlers. The forest's extensive network of backcountry trails will get you around a landscape dotted with highland bogs and dense thickets of blueberries. Black bears, foxes, beavers, woodchucks, opossums, and mink are among the mammals found in Monongahela. There are also dozens of types of fish in the streams, more than 200 feathered species in the skies and the treetops, and 75 types of trees rooted in the forest's fertile soil.

The Monongahela National Forest covers 919,000 rugged acres.

HARPERS FERRY

The town of Harpers Ferry, West Virginia, at the confluence of the Shenandoah and Potomac rivers, is best known for abolitionist John Brown's raid on an arsenal in 1859. He believed that with the weapons stored there, the slaves could fight for their own freedom. When the Civil War ended, Harpers Ferry became a focal point during Reconstruction. The town made many early attempts at integrating former slaves into society. This included the 1867 establishment of Storer College, one of the first integrated schools in the United States.

Now designated Harpers Ferry National Historical Park, the West Virginia town and surrounding areas in Virginia and Maryland create a popular way station for hikers traveling the Appalachian Trail. Harpers Ferry offers historical re-creations, but visitors also come to fish, raft, hike, and explore.

(Top right) **Harpers Ferry**, West Virginia, is a small but historically important town at the confluence of the Potomac and Shenandoah rivers. The town has a population just below 300.

(Bottom right) **The New River Gorge Bridge** is one of the most photographed places in West Virginia.

OTHER WEST VIRGINIA ATTRACTIONS

- Hawks Nest State Park (Fayette County)
- Gauley River National Recreation Area (Summersville)
- New River Gorge (Fayette, Raleigh, Summers counties)
- Bluestone State Park (Summers County)
- Blackwater Falls State Park (Davis)
- Seneca Caverns (Riverton)
- Cass Scenic Railroad State Park (Cass)
- West Virginia State Capitol (Charleston)

KENTUCKY

KENTUCKY DERBY

It's called "the most exciting two minutes in sports" and features 20 world-class athletes culled from a field of more than 30,000. The athletes in question are three-year-old thoroughbred horses. The winner covers the 1.25-mile track at Churchill Downs in Louisville, Kentucky, in just about two minutes at a gallop averaging almost 40 miles per hour.

The first "jewel" of the three races collectively known as the Triple Crown, the Kentucky Derby is no ordinary sporting event. Run every May since 1875, the Derby is a raucous party, a longstanding tradition, and a vibrant pageant.

More than 150,000 people attend the Derby each year. "Millionaire's Row," frequented by VIPs, is one place from which spectators can view the action. Another spot is the infield; this area is much rowdier and muddier and can hold up to 80,000 people.

MAMMOTH CAVE

Mammoth Cave, the world's longest known network of caverns, is hidden below the forested hills of southern Kentucky. There are more than 350 miles of underground passages on five different levels.

Mammoth Cave is made up of limestone, which dissolves when water seeps through the ground. As the water works its way downward, the limestone erodes, forming the honeycomb of underground passageways, amphitheaters, and rooms that make up Mammoth Cave. Mammoth Cave National Park preserves the cave system and a part of the Green River valley.

The dazzling array of stalagmites, stalactites, and columns of **Mammoth Cave** are the product of water seeping downward for many millennia.

(Above) You can see one of the most famous natural sandstone arches in Kentucky at **Natural Bridge State Resort Park** in Slade. The "Natural Bridge" is 65 feet tall and 78 feet long.

KENTUCKY PLACES TO VISIT

- National Quilt Museum (Paducah)
- Smothers Park (Owensboro)
- Kentucky Horse Park (Lexington)
- Mary Todd Lincoln House (Lexington)
- Shaker Village of Pleasant Hill (Harrodsburg)
- Cumberland Falls State Resort Park (Corbin)
- Conrad-Caldwell House Museum (Louisville)
- Louisville Palace (Louisville)

LOUISVILLE SLUGGER MUSEUM & FACTORY

Ever since Bud Hillerich created the first Louisville Slugger bat in his father's workshop in 1884, baseball's biggest stars have used these finely crafted pieces of smooth white ash. A collection of famous bats lines the walls of the Louisville Slugger Museum & Factory; most notable is the 1927 Louisville Slugger bat Babe Ruth used to hit 21 home runs. You can still see the notches carved by Ruth himself on the top of the bat. Take the factory tour to learn about the steps used to make the bats, from the massive beginnings to the completed varnish.

(Top right) The world's largest bat, a 120-foot-tall replica of Babe Ruth's, leans against the **Louisville Slugger Museum & Factory** near its entrance. Nearby you'll also find the world's largest baseball glove.

TENNESSEE

BEALE STREET

Beale Street, in Memphis, Tennessee, is truly a multisensory experience. Pots of gumbo and red beans and rice simmer at every corner, but the smells and tastes of Beale Street are just side dishes. The main course is the music played at the neon-and-brick clubs.

Memphis touts itself as the "Birthplace of Rock 'n' Roll," and it's got a strong case for the title. In the mid-1950s, Memphis's blues legacy fused with country music, creating a new sound that found fans across the country. Beale Street has remained the heart and soul of music in Memphis.

In the early 20th century, **Beale Street** was one of the busiest markets in the South. In the 1980s, Beale Street was redeveloped into an open-air, pedestrian-only center for music and nightlife.

NATIONAL CIVIL RIGHTS MUSEUM

This Memphis, Tennessee, museum chronicles the history of civil rights activities from the beginnings of slavery through the end of the 20th century. The museum focuses on such events as the Civil War, the Supreme Court decision to desegregate schools, the lunch counter sit-ins, the Montgomery Bus Boycott, and the March on Washington.

The National Civil Rights Museum was built around the Lorraine Motel, where Dr. Martin Luther King Jr. was assassinated in 1968.

Exhibits at the **National Civil Rights Museum** include a restored public bus like the one ridden by Rosa Parks when she refused to move to the back seats.

Graceland is now on the national register of historic places, and it has become a magnet for Elvis fans everywhere. Elvis's house attracts upward of 750,000 fans a year.

PLACES TO SEE IN TENNESSEE

- The Parthenon (Nashville)
- Dollywood (Pigeon Forge)
- Andrew Jackson's Hermitage (Hermitage)
- Shiloh National Military Park (Shiloh)
- Fort Donelson National Battlefield (Dover)
- Andrew Johnson National Historic Site (Greeneville)
- Museum of Appalachia (Clinton)

GRACELAND

Elvis Presley bought Graceland mansion in Memphis, Tennessee's Whitehaven neighborhood in 1957 when he was just 22 years old. He paid $102,500 for the property, an 18-room mansion on nearly 14 acres of country estate surrounded by towering oak trees. Corinthian columns and a limestone façade mark the exterior of the home. The interior has been preserved as it was at the time of Elvis's death in 1977. Elvis's legendary taste included his so-called "Jungle Room," replete with an in-wall waterfall and green shag carpeting on the floor and ceiling; his eclectic billiards parlor, plastered in yards of ornately patterned fabric; and his TV room, with a yellow, white, and blue color scheme and three television sets Presley watched simultaneously.

GRAND OLE OPRY

The Grand Ole Opry in Nashville, Tennessee, is a cultural phenomenon. At its heart, it's a radio program that showcases American country music. In fact, it's the longest-running live radio program in the United States.

But country music is just the starting point. The Opry is the centerpiece of Opryland, a comprehensive resort and convention center that offers everything from golf to shopping to, of course, country music.

(Left) Shows at the **Grand Ole Opry** are magical to the performers and audience alike.

GREAT SMOKY MOUNTAINS NATIONAL PARK

Shrouded in thick forest along the border of North Carolina and Tennessee, the Great Smoky Mountains are the United States' highest range east of South Dakota's Black Hills. The park often feels like a vestige of an ancient era when trees ruled the planet. Today, more than 100 species of trees and 1,300 varieties of flowering plants grow in the park. The respiration of all this plant life produces the gauzy haze that gives the mountains their "smoky" name.

The park's highest point is the 6,643-foot peak of **Clingman's Dome**. On clear days, you can see as far as 100 miles from the top of its observation tower.

GEORGIA

SAVANNAH

Savannah, Georgia, is America's first planned city. General James Edward Oglethorpe (who had previously founded the colony of Georgia) founded Savannah in 1733. He designed his new capital as a series of neighborhoods centered around 24 squares. His layout remains intact today. Each square has a distinctive architecture, history, and folklore.

(Above) **Johnson Square,** laid out in 1733, was the first square in Savannah.

(Above) **Chippewa Square** is at the center of the downtown historic district. A statue of General Oglethorpe at the square commemorates the founding of Georgia. The square gets its name from the Battle of Chippewa in the War of 1812.

PLACES TO VISIT IN SAVANNAH

- Old Fort James Jackson
- Bonaventure Cemetery
- Leopold's Ice Cream
- Forsyth Park
- River Street
- Owens-Thomas House
- Cathedral of St. John the Baptist
- Juliette Gordon Low Birthplace
- Fort Pulaski National Monument
- Wormsloe Historic Site

TYBEE ISLAND

Eighteen miles east of Savannah, Georgia, Tybee Island is an exclusive beach getaway with plenty of opportunities to relax and sightsee. Visit this barrier island's three-mile beach. Enjoy boat cruises, fishing trips, or kayaking. Venture into the salt marshes to go bird-watching. Or check out local marine life on display at the Tybee Island Marine Science Center. There are also biking and hiking trails across the island.

(Below) The **Tybee Island Lighthouse** is the oldest and tallest lighthouse in Georgia. First constructed in 1736, the lighthouse stands 144 feet high.

AMICALOLA FALLS

A hiker's paradise unfolds at Amicalola Falls State Park in Georgia as 12 miles of trails weave through the picturesque Appalachian Mountains and lead to the Amicalola Watershed and Amicalola Falls. At 729 feet, Amicalola Falls is the tallest waterfall in Georgia and one of the tallest east of the Mississippi River. Its name means "Tumbling Waters" in Cherokee.

(Above) Herds of wild horses roam **Cumberland Island**. It's said Spanish explorers left them behind in the 16th century.

CUMBERLAND ISLAND

Cumberland Island is Georgia's largest and southernmost barrier island. The remote island is 3 miles wide and is ringed by a beach almost 18 miles long. It's covered by acres of marsh, tidal creeks, sand dunes, blinding white sand, and historic ruins and museums that compel admiration and amazement.

GOLDEN ISLES OF GEORGIA

The Golden Isles of Georgia are a group of four barrier islands—St. Simons Island, Sea Island, Jekyll Island, and Little St. Simons Island. All have stunning beaches, as well as marshes and creeks that are great fun to explore by canoe or kayak.

ST. SIMONS ISLAND

St. Simons Island is the largest and most developed of the Golden Isles. It measures 45 square miles and boasts many beautiful old homes and estates. The island offers great fishing and inviting beaches.

(Right) **St. Simons Island** is home to one of the nation's oldest continually working lighthouses open to visitors.

(Below) The **Jekyll Island Club** is a local landmark and an elegant resort.

MARTIN LUTHER KING JR. NATIONAL HISTORICAL PARK

The Martin Luther King Jr. National Historical Park in Atlanta consists of several sites central to the civil rights leader's early life, his later work, and his place of worship. These sites include the birth home, the "I Have a Dream" World Peace Rose Garden, the King Center, and the historic Ebenezer Baptist Church.

(Top) Dr. King's birthplace and boyhood home in the heart of Atlanta's "Sweet Auburn" district (the city's prosperous African American downtown in segregated days) is part of the **Martin Luther King Jr. National Historical Park**.

JEKYLL ISLAND

Jekyll Island is Georgia's smallest barrier island and lies off the coast midway between Savannah, Georgia, and Jacksonville, Florida. Jekyll Island was a popular destination for the country's rich and powerful and is now a favorite among those looking for a relaxing beach getaway.

NORTH CAROLINA

CAPE HATTERAS

Hatteras is a largely untamed string of barrier islands about 70 miles long. The dunes, marshes, and woodlands that mark the thin strand of land between North Carolina's coastal sounds and the Atlantic Ocean are a diverse ecosystem defined by the wind and the sea.

Countless shipwrecks earned Cape Hatteras a treacherous reputation and the nickname "The Graveyard of the Atlantic." The navigational dangers led to the construction of several lighthouses, including Cape Hatteras Lighthouse and Ocracoke Lighthouse (built in 1823, it's the oldest operating lighthouse in North Carolina).

Although crowds are few and far between, Cape Hatteras is a popular recreational destination. Try the waters on each side of the island—they are considered some of the best on the entire East Coast for surfing and fishing.

The 208-foot-tall **Cape Hatteras Lighthouse** is the tallest in the United States. Visitors may climb the 268 steps to its top for a commanding view of the shoreline.

BILTMORE ESTATE

The Biltmore mansion is the centerpiece of an immaculate 8,000-acre estate that includes lush gardens, active vineyards, and a luxury inn. It was the vision of George W. Vanderbilt. In the late 1880s, he purchased 125,000 acres in the Blue Ridge Mountains near Asheville, North Carolina, where he built the 250-room French Renaissance château.

Originally the country retreat of the Vanderbilt family, **Biltmore** has evolved into a swanky tourist attraction.

BLUE RIDGE PARKWAY

"America's Favorite Drive" glides along the ridgetops of the southern Appalachian mountainside. The peaks are more than 6,000 feet above sea level, offering remarkable views of the verdant fields and country towns far below.

The Blue Ridge Parkway winds 469 miles from Shenandoah National Park to Great Smoky Mountains National Park.

Elizabeth II, docked at Manteo Harbor on Roanoke Island, is a composite design modeled after the original *Elizabeth*, one of the ships that sailed to the New World in 1585.

PLACES TO VISIT

- Outer Banks
- Chimney Rock State Park (Chimney Rock)
- Linville Gorge Wilderness (Burke County)
- Hanging Rock State Park (Stokes County)
- Grandfather Mountain (near Linville)
- Battleship North Carolina (Wilmington)
- Great Smoky Mountains National Park

ROANOKE ISLAND

In 1587, Sir Walter Raleigh of England sent an expedition to Roanoke Island, a 27-acre isle off what is now the North Carolina coast. About 116 settlers sailed across the Atlantic and established a village there. But they arrived too late in the year to plant crops, and their leader, John White, returned to England for supplies. White couldn't return to Roanoke Island until 1590. When he arrived, the village was deserted. Roanoke became known as the "Lost Colony." The mystery remains unsolved.

Modern Roanoke Island is home to a historic park that tells this story and others through living-history demonstrations, a replica of a 16th-century sailing ship, and an interactive museum. Boardwalks and nature trails reveal native wildflowers and protected maritime forest. An outdoor pavilion hosts a performing arts series.

SOUTH CAROLINA

MYRTLE BEACH

South Carolina's Grand Strand, Myrtle Beach, has been a favorite sun-and-sand destination for more than a century. The beach is named for the numerous wax myrtle trees growing along the shore. The Seaside Inn, which opened in 1901, became the first of many increasingly sophisticated resorts that have made this one of the top tourist areas on the East Coast.

Myrtle Beach is known for its great family atmosphere, thanks to a lively boardwalk and numerous waterfront tourist attractions, including an amusement park.

The **Harbour Town Yacht Basin** is a favorite attraction on Hilton Head Island.

HILTON HEAD ISLAND

Hilton Head Island is one of the premier destinations in the Southeast. The barrier island's pristine natural environment is balanced with the graceful aesthetics of some of the finest resorts and golf courses. The combination is a magnet for visitors: Although the year-round population is just over 37,000, Hilton Head Island sees about 2.5 million tourists each year. They come not only for the lush scenery, posh resorts, and great golf, but also for the fresh coastal air, abundant peace and quiet, and the beautiful sunsets.

History buffs will enjoy a tour of **Fort Sumter National Monument**, located off the coast near Charleston, where the first shots of the Civil War were fired.

SOUTH CAROLINA PLACES TO VISIT

- Congaree National Park (Hopkins)
- Boone Hall Plantation (Mount Pleasant)
- Pinckney Island National Wildlife Refuge (near Hilton Head Island)
- Middleton Place (near Charleston)
- Huntington Beach State Park (near Murrells Inlet)
- South Carolina State Museum (Columbia)
- Riverbanks Zoo and Garden (Columbia)
- Caesars Head State Park (Greenville County)

Magnolia Plantation and Gardens is a great example of Charleston's preservation. You can tour the home and take the Nature Train tour to see the plantation's many animals, including alligators.

CHARLESTON

Charleston, South Carolina, is a beautifully preserved city full of antebellum mansions, quaint cobblestone alleys, and carefully preserved historic buildings. After the Civil War devastated the community, residents were so poor that they could not afford to rebuild, so the city simply adapted its old buildings, unknowingly protecting them as historical treasures for future generations to appreciate.

FLORIDA

EVERGLADES NATIONAL PARK

This national treasure at the southern tip of Florida encompasses 1.5 million acres of saw grass marshes, tangled mangrove forests, and fresh and brackish water wetlands. Tram tours and hiking trails are available in areas of the Everglades open to the public. However, this slow-moving "River of Grass" is best explored by boat. At Flamingo Marina you can rent a kayak, a canoe, or a skiff to see an incredible collection of animals up close. Gorgeous fish, turtles, marsh rabbits, manatees, crocodiles, otters, alligators, and hundreds of species of birds inhabit the park. If you are very lucky, you might even spot a rare Florida panther.

The Florida Everglades is the only place on Earth where crocodiles and alligators native to the U.S. naturally coexist.

High-speed airboats, propelled by fanlike contraptions, are a fun way to tour the swampy marshes of this unique wetland. Many outfitters offer guided airboat tours.

Everglades National Park offers a number of easy boardwalk trails for those who want to explore on foot. **The Anhinga Trail** is one of the park's most dependable areas for wildlife viewing.

JOHN F. KENNEDY SPACE CENTER

The John F. Kennedy Space Center in Cape Canaveral has been the launch site for all crewed U.S. space missions since 1962. Tours offered at the Kennedy Space Center give an in-depth behind-the-scenes look at NASA, including visits to launch pads and rockets. Cape Canaveral is also home to the Canaveral National Seashore and the Merritt Island National Wildlife Refuge.

The Rocket Garden at the John F. Kennedy Space Center gives visitors an up-close look at the rockets and capsules that first launched NASA astronauts into space.

Novelist Ernest Hemingway wrote many of his best works while on the island, and today **Hemingway House** is Key West's top tourist attraction.

KEY WEST

Key West has long been famous as one of America's top destinations for fun-and-sun vacations. Key West has retained its charm, remoteness, intriguing history, natural beauty, and idyllic weather (except during hurricane season) since the 1920s. Mallory Square hosts the Sunset Celebration each evening, with food vendors, fire-eaters, tightrope walkers, and arts and crafts exhibits.

ST. AUGUSTINE

St. Augustine, Florida, is the oldest permanently inhabited city in the United States. Founded in 1565, it's filled with reminders of its early Spanish history. Walking through the carefully restored Spanish Quarter, you'll see narrow cobblestone streets, the oldest wooden schoolhouse in the country, and Ponce de Leon's Fountain of Youth.

CASTILLO DE SAN MARCOS

Castillo de San Marcos and its 25 acres of old parade grounds are a must-see on any visit to St. Augustine. The fortress, built by Spaniards between 1672 and 1695, boasts an impressive moat, a drawbridge, and huge cannons atop which kids can sit. Castillo de San Marcos once helped guard St. Augustine from pirate raids. Later, supporters of the American Revolution were locked away in its dank and creepy dungeons.

(Top and bottom right) The walls of **Castillo de San Marcos** are made of a durable substance called coquina (a limestone material composed of broken seashells and coral), which helped the fort remain impenetrable.

FLORIDA PLACES TO VISIT

- Big Cypress National Reserve (Ochopee)
- Fort Matanzas (St. Augustine)
- Dry Tortugas (Key West)
- De Soto National Memorial (Bradenton)
- Art Deco District of South Beach (Miami)
- Little Havana neighborhood (Miami)
- Sanibel Island (south of Fort Myers)
- Destin (Florida's Emerald Coast)

RINGLING ESTATE

Circus owner and art collector John Ringling and his wife, Mable, began building their Italian Renaissance-style mansion in Sarasota Bay, Florida, in 1924. The building was named Cà d'Zan, meaning "House of John" in Venetian dialect. A 60-foot tower caps the mansion. An impressive 8,000-square-foot marble terrace offers awe-inspiring views of Sarasota Bay.

The estate also contains the John and Mable Ringling Museum of Art. Their art treasures include more than 10,000 paintings, sculptures, drawings, prints, photographs, and decorative arts. The museum holds the largest private collection of paintings and drawings by Peter Paul Rubens.

ALABAMA

VULCAN STATUE

The 56-foot statue of Vulcan in Birmingham, Alabama, is the largest cast-iron statue in the world. The creation of the sculpture is tied closely to the roots of the city. Birmingham began as a mining town for coal, limestone, and iron ore, which were forged to make steel. By the 20th century, it was a formidable industrial power. The city's business leaders, seeking to promote Birmingham, had Italian sculptor Giuseppe Moretti create a cast-iron sculpture of Vulcan, the Roman god of fire, volcanoes, and the forge. The sculpture was unveiled at the 1904 St. Louis World's Fair, where it was a hit.

When the statue was moved back to Birmingham, its arms were reassembled improperly. The statue was neglected and became a three-dimensional billboard. In 1939, Vulcan was finally moved to his proper place on Birmingham's Red Mountain. Restoration of the statue was completed in 2004, and Vulcan Park reopened for the statue's centennial. Today the statue provides a panoramic view of Birmingham.

PLACES TO VISIT IN ALABAMA

- Gulf State Park (Baldwin County)
- Fort Morgan (Mobile Bay)
- Birmingham Civil Rights Institute (Birmingham)
- Birmingham Museum of Art (Birmingham)
- Frank Lloyd Wright Rosenbaum House Museum (Florence)
- Little River Canyon National Preserve (Fort Payne)
- Cheaha State Park (Clay and Cleburne counties)
- USS *Alabama* Battleship Memorial Park (Mobile)

The cast-iron **Vulcan Statue** in Birmingham has been restored to symbolize the town's steel history.

GULF COAST OF ALABAMA

Alabama's Gulf Coast has 32 miles of white sand beaches and water warm enough to swim in eight months of the year. The towns of Gulf Shores and Orange Beach offer plenty of accommodations lining the shore and family fun such as miniature golf, water parks, marinas, and ice cream parlors.

The fine, white sand on the beaches of **Gulf Shores** on the Alabama Gulf Coast must have inspired the phrase "white sugar sand."

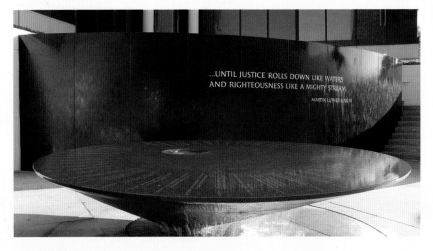

The Civil Rights Memorial in Montgomery, Alabama, records the names of the people who died in the struggle for civil rights and chronicles the history of the movement. The adjacent Civil Rights Memorial Center displays exhibits about Civil Rights Movement martyrs.

The U.S. Space and Rocket Center showcases the hardware used in the space program and houses a multitude of artifacts.

U.S. SPACE AND ROCKET CENTER

The U.S. Space and Rocket Center in Huntsville, Alabama, showcases a fascinating and comprehensive collection of rockets, missiles, boosters, and space memorabilia. On display are capsules and space suits used over the years in NASA missions and a mock-up of *Saturn V*, the 363-foot rocket that helped launch astronauts to the moon. There's also a full-size mock-up of a space shuttle and a lunar rover vehicle.

MISSISSIPPI

NATCHEZ TRACE

Natchez Trace originated thousands of years ago. Big animals such as deer and bison were the first to tramp along what became the Old Natchez Trace. Then the Choctaw and Chickasaw connected the paths, and the trail became the region's premiere trade route. Arriving Europeans grasped its potential, and by the late 1700s the Natchez Trace bustled with boaters. They would sell their cargo and flatboats or keelboats for lumber in Natchez or New Orleans and then travel back north to Nashville and beyond. In 1801, the United States signed a treaty with the Choctaw allowing roads to be built along the route.

Today, the 444-mile Natchez Trace Parkway is a recreational and scenic drive that runs from Natchez, Mississippi, to just outside Nashville, Tennessee. Adventurers can enjoy numerous hiking trails, archeological sites, scenic overlooks, recreational activities, waterfalls, picnic sites, and campgrounds along the parkway.

Natchez Trace, which runs from Mississippi to Tennessee, began as a series of tribal trading routes.

GULF ISLANDS NATIONAL SEASHORE

From above, the Gulf Islands National Seashore looks like a sandy string of pearls off the coasts of Florida and Mississippi. Along the water are miles of snow-white beaches, bayous, saltwater marshes, maritime forests, nature trails, and barrier islands. West Ship Island is located 12 miles south of the Mississippi coastline and is one of the islands included in the national seashore. Tour boats carry visitors to the island, where motorized vehicles are not allowed.

Visitors to West Ship Island can tour historic **Fort Massachusetts**, which played a role in the Civil War. You can still see the immense 300-pound cannons that were installed in 1874.

The white sand of **Gulf Islands National Seashore** is believed to have eroded from rocky areas to the north.

These Corinthian columns are all that remains of the **Windsor Mansion**, a large Greek Revival house that was built for Smith Coffee Daniel II in Claiborne County. The mansion stood from 1861 to 1890, when it was destroyed by fire.

MISSISSIPPI PLACES TO VISIT

- Delta Blues Festival (Greenville)
- Old Capitol Museum (Jackson)
- Mississippi Civil Rights Museum (Jackson)
- Rock & Blues Heritage Museum (Clarksdale)
- Elvis Presley Birthplace (Tupelo)
- Tupelo Automobile Museum (Tupelo)
- Natchez National Historical Park (Natchez)
- B.B. King Museum and Delta Interpretive Center (Indianola)
- Vicksburg National Military Park and Cemetery (Vicksburg)
- Old Courthouse Museum (Vicksburg)

Clark Creek Natural Area is a 700-acre state park that features some 50 waterfalls. The park is great for hiking and bird-watching.

ARKANSAS

BLANCHARD SPRINGS CAVERNS

Blanchard Springs Caverns in north-central Arkansas is the jewel of the Ozarks. This three-level cave system has almost every kind of cave formation: from soda straws to bacon formations to rimstone cave pools. The most famous formation in these caverns is the 70-foot-high joined stalagmite-stalactite called the Giant Column.

Visitors can choose from three scenic trails through Blanchard Springs Caverns. The Dripstone Trail is a one-hour trail around the upper level that is stroller- and wheelchair-accessible. The Discovery Trail is a longer section that winds through the middle level. If you're looking for a challenge, the four-hour Wild Cave Tour is an introduction to spelunking requiring athleticism, endurance, and equipment available by reservation only.

The shimmering **Ghost Room** is a highlight of the Discovery Trail.

After a long day of hiking in the Ozarks, the **Hot Springs bathhouses** offer a relaxing soak for the weary traveler.

HOT SPRINGS NATIONAL PARK

Hot Springs National Park protects 47 different hot springs and their watershed on Hot Springs Mountain, as well as the eight historic bathhouses in the town of Hot Springs, Arkansas. For more than 200 years, vacationers have come to the waters in bathhouse row in hopes of curing all kinds of ills, and tourists can still enjoy a soak in several bathhouses. But there's much more to Hot Springs National Park than a relaxing soak. Favorite recreations include hiking, crystal prospecting, camping in Gulpha Gorge Campground, and driving or hiking up Hot Springs Mountain to enjoy the 40-mile view from Hot Springs Tower.

ARKANSAS PLACES TO VISIT

- Ozark Folk Center State Park (near Mountain View)
- Little Rock Central High School National Historic Site (Little Rock)
- William J. Clinton Presidential Library and Museum (Little Rock)
- Pea Ridge National Military Park (Pea Ridge)
- Ouachita National Forest (Western Arkansas)
- Arkansas Air Museum (Fayetteville)
- Crater of Diamonds State Park (Murfreesboro)

Enjoy the wide-open serenity of the **Ozark National Forest.** There are campsites and opportunities for fishing, hiking, and watching wildlife.

Petit Jean State Park lies between the Ozark and the Ouachita Mountain ranges in west-central Arkansas. The park contains more than 3,000 acres of woods, ravines, streams, waterfalls, stunning views, and surprising geological formations.

Buffalo National River is one of the few remaining undammed rivers in the contiguous United States. The 135-mile river contains both swift-moving rapids and calm pools and flows through the Ozark Mountains.

LOUISIANA

PLANTATION ALLEY

Louisiana's Great River Road is also known as Plantation Alley. There, 30 antebellum mansions and 10 other ancient properties sit regally on bluffs overlooking the Mississippi River. All are open for tours or have been converted into hotels or bed-and-breakfast inns. Along the Great River Road, they provide a dignified procession of antebellum architecture surrounded by sugarcane fields and pecan groves. To tour Plantation Alley, start in Baton Rouge, and drive south. Instead of taking I-10 straight to New Orleans, travel along the Mississippi River toward Plaquemine, White Castle, and Donaldsonville.

The well-known **Houmas House** in Burnside was once the center of a 20,000-acre sugarcane plantation. This Greek Revival mansion is furnished with antiques.

Oak Alley Plantation is a sweeping columned mansion framed by live oaks. It has been the setting for movies including *Interview with the Vampire* and *Primary Colors*.

LOUISIANA'S GREAT RIVER ROAD PLANTATIONS INCLUDE:

- Oak Alley Plantation (Vacherie)
- Laura Plantation (Vacherie)
- St. Joseph Plantation (Vacherie)
- Nottoway Plantation (White Castle)
- Houmas House (Burnside)
- San Francisco Plantation (Garyville)
- Destrehan Plantation (Destrehan)

The Old State Capitol in Baton Rouge is one of the premier examples of Gothic-revival architecture in the United States. The building is now a museum.

MARDI GRAS

Now the biggest annual party in North America, New Orleans's Carnival is an over-the-top street party that typically attracts more than a million people from all over the world. Carnival culminates with Mardi Gras, or Fat Tuesday, the wild event that turns New Orleans into a center of celebration.

The parades are the flamboyant soul of Carnival. Each parade is organized by a group called a krewe. Each krewe selects a king and queen to reign over the parade. Elaborate multicolor floats carry krewe members in ornate costumes.

New Orleans's famous **French Quarter**—in particular, Bourbon Street—becomes a wild party during Carnival.

ILLINOIS

MILLENNIUM PARK

What was once an eyesore of decaying railroad tracks and parking lots near Chicago's lakefront is now a stunning 24.5-acre urban jewel called Millennium Park. Among its major attractions are two pieces of public art: *Cloud Gate* and the *Crown Fountain*. The highly reflective 110-ton polished steel sculpture officially named *Cloud Gate* is affectionately called "The Bean." Visitors can see the park and cityscape reflected in its curves. The *Crown Fountain* is a reflecting pool flanked by two 50-foot towers onto which close-up images of Chicagoans are projected. The faces smile, laugh, and squirt water, much to the delight of onlookers. On warm days, children splash in the shallow water between the two towers. Other attractions include the Lurie Garden and the Jay Pritzker Pavilion. A large outdoor ice-skating rink is open throughout the winter months.

(Above) The *Crown Fountain* is made up of glass blocks erected in front of two gigantic video screens. The screens display a continuous loop of faces that smile, laugh, and spray water.

(Below) A 12-foot-high arch forms the "gate" in the highly polished *Cloud Gate* sculpture.

WRIGLEY FIELD

The Chicago Cubs and their fans prize their quaint home ballpark, Wrigley Field. Wrigley was built in 1914 for $250,000 and featured baseball's first permanent concession stand. It's the second-oldest major league park, next to Fenway Park in Boston. Grab a ticket, hot dog, and beer and sit among the famous Bleacher Bums. Afterward, join the untiring Cubs fans at neighborhood bars and restaurants just steps from Wrigley.

THE ART INSTITUTE OF CHICAGO

The Art Institute of Chicago boasts more than 300,000 works, including treasured paintings such as Edward Hopper's "Nighthawks," Grant Wood's "American Gothic," and Georges Seurat's "A Sunday on La Grand Jatte." The Art Institute's collections of early Italian, Dutch, Flemish, and Spanish works include paintings by El Greco, Hals, Rembrandt, and Goya. It also features one of the largest collections of Monet's works. The striking Italian-Renaissance architecture gives the building a distinctive look among downtown Chicago's skyscrapers.

This stately lion is one of two that guard the entrance to the **Art Institute**.

NAVY PIER

Chicago's lakefront playground is a fabulous 50-acre complex of parks, promenades, shops, and restaurants. Much of it really is a pier overhanging the waters of Lake Michigan. Navy Pier's most visible attraction is a 150-foot-high Ferris wheel that was modeled after the one built for Chicago's 1893 World Columbian Exposition. It's a great way to get a bird's-eye view of the area and the city's spectacular skyline.

The original **Navy Pier**, once called Municipal Pier, dates back to 1914 and was once used as a naval training base. Today, it's alive with activity.

The library opened in 2004, the museum in 2005. Only six months after it opened, the museum welcomed its 400,000th visitor—a record for presidential libraries.

ABRAHAM LINCOLN PRESIDENTIAL LIBRARY AND MUSEUM

The Abraham Lincoln Presidential Library and Museum in Springfield, Illinois, combines scholarship and showmanship to sweep visitors along from Lincoln's humble beginnings in a log cabin to his presidency during the Civil War. Replicas of Lincoln's boyhood home, the Lincoln White House, and his box at Ford's Theatre give an aura of realism to the exhibits.

PLACES TO VISIT IN ILLINOIS

- Willis Tower (Chicago)
- Chicago Blues Festival (Chicago)
- Museum of Science and Industry (Chicago)
- Cave-in-Rock State Park (Hardin County, Southern Illinois)
- Ferne Clyffe State Park (Johnson County, Southern Illinois)
- Cahokia Mounds State Historic Site (Collinsville)
- Ulysses S. Grant Home State Historic Site (Galena)
- Dana-Thomas House (Springfield)
- Anderson Japanese Gardens (Rockford)

The **Shawnee National Forest** consists of approximately 280,000 acres in the hills of Southern Illinois. The Garden of the Gods (below) is one of several wilderness areas within the Shawnee National Forest.

Located along the bank of the Illinois River in LaSalle County, **Starved Rock State Park** offers 13 miles of trails, spectacular waterfalls, canyon views, and fishing in the Illinois River.

INDIANA

INDIANAPOLIS 500

Named for the number of miles covered by circling the 2.5-mile track 200 times, the Indianapolis 500 occurs every year at the Indianapolis Motor Speedway, also known as the Brickyard. The race has been held during Memorial Day weekend every year since 1911, with the exception of six years during World Wars I and II. It is one of the longest-standing and richest motorsports events in the world.

Many 500-goers are more interested in partying than watching the race. On race day, the track's infield hosts a tailgate party of epic proportions. The track infield also holds a museum, part of an 18-hole golf course, concert stages, corporate "tent parties," and just about everything else one could shoehorn into a couple hundred acres of former farmland.

The Indianapolis Motor Speedway, also called the Brickyard, is the famed home of the Indianapolis 500.

The popular Dinosphere exhibit at the **Children's Museum of Indianapolis** immerses children in the cretaceous period of more than 65 million years ago and lets them examine actual fossils.

CHILDREN'S MUSEUM OF INDIANAPOLIS

This world-class collection of hands-on fun makes up the largest children's museum in the world. Its exhibits continue to amaze and entertain local children, as well as families who make the trek to the city just to visit this renowned attraction.

(Below) **The Lanier Mansion State Historic Site** in Madison, Indiana, is recognized as a masterpiece of the Greek Revival style. The house was built for banker James Franklin Doughty Lanier in 1844 and designed by architect Francis Costigan.

(Above) **Indiana Dunes National Lakeshore** runs 15 miles along the southern shore of Lake Michigan. More than 50 miles of hiking trails take you through dunes, wetlands, prairies, rivers, and forests.

(Above) **Brown County State Park,** located in Southern Indiana, offers many trails for hiking and horseback riding. Visitors can also enjoy fishing or ice fishing on the park's two lakes.

OHIO

ROCK AND ROLL HALL OF FAME

Rock 'n' roll lives on today, more than a half-century after its birth. One reason is Cleveland's Rock and Roll Hall of Fame and Museum. Designed by architect I. M. Pei, the building expresses the raw power of rock music. The geometric and cantilevered forms are often compared to a turntable. The striking building and its 162-foot tower anchor Cleveland's North Coast Harbor.

The hall began operation in 1986 with the ceremonial induction of its first class of rock stars: Chuck Berry, Elvis Presley, Little Richard, Sam Cooke, the Everly Brothers, and Buddy Holly, among others. It holds a collection of rock memorabilia and rarities and features groundbreaking exhibitions.

The Rock and Roll Hall of Fame is the world's first museum honoring rock music.

Originally the Union Terminal train station, the building reopened as the **Cincinnati Museum Center** in 1990.

CINCINNATI MUSEUM CENTER

The Cincinnati Museum Center at Union Terminal is an art deco masterwork that attracts visitors from around the world. Union Terminal was an architectural icon since it opened in 1933, but after train travel dwindled, the terminal was declared a National Historic Landmark in 1977 and stood empty for more than a decade. Today the terminal is home to five major Cincinnati cultural organizations: the Cincinnati History Museum, the Duke Energy Children's Museum, the Museum of Natural History & Science, the Robert D. Lindner Family OMNIMAX Theater, and the Cincinnati Historical Library and Archives.

PLACES TO VISIT IN OHIO

- Cleveland Museum of Art (Cleveland)
- Stan Hywet Hall and Gardens (Akron)
- Pro Football Hall of Fame (Canton)
- Dayton Aviation Heritage National Historic Park (Dayton)
- Franklin Park Conservatory and Botanical Garden (Columbus)
- National Underground Railroad Freedom Center (Cincinnati)
- Serpent Mound (Adams County, Southern Ohio)
- Cedar Point amusement park (Sandusky)

(Above) **Hocking Hills State Park** contains spectacular rock formations, waterfalls, and caves.

CUYAHOGA VALLEY NATIONAL PARK

Cuyahoga Valley National Park, which lies between Akron and Cleveland in Ohio, may be the park service's most urban-friendly environment. The park preserves 33,000 acres along the Cuyahoga River, called "crooked river" by the Mohawk Indians. The forests, plains, streams, and ravines here contain an astonishing array of fauna and flora, not to mention a variety of recreational opportunities. The park has almost no roads, but you can explore plenty of bike and hiking paths. Don't miss the cultural exhibits and events, such as historic displays and outdoor concerts.

(Below) Probably the most-photographed feature of Cuyahoga Valley National Park is **Brandywine Falls**. The 60-foot-high falls are approachable by boardwalk.

MICHIGAN

ISLE ROYALE NATIONAL PARK

Isle Royale, which was carved and compressed by glaciers, is the largest island on Lake Superior. It exists in splendid isolation—you can only get to the island by boat, seaplane, or ferry. Together with numerous smaller islands it makes up Isle Royale National Park, located off of Michigan's Upper Peninsula. There are no roads on the island, but you can choose routes from among the 165 miles of hiking trails. Diving for shipwrecks is another favorite activity—there are more than ten major wrecks below the surface of the lake.

(Below) **The Rock Harbor Lighthouse** at the northeast end of Isle Royale was built in 1855.

PICTURED ROCKS NATIONAL LAKESHORE

Pictured Rocks National Lakeshore spans 42 miles of Lake Superior shoreline, covering more than 73,000 acres of Michigan's Upper Peninsula. It is a preserve of spectacular scenery and cascading sand dunes. Despite the remote location, almost 400,000 visitors each year seek out Pictured Rocks for hunting, fishing, hiking, and boating in summer and spring. In fall and winter, snowshoeing, snowmobiling, ice fishing, and cross-country skiing are popular.

MACKINAC BRIDGE

The mighty Mackinac Bridge straddles the Straits of Mackinac between Lakes Michigan and Huron to connect Michigan's upper and lower peninsulas. Pronounced *MA keh nah,* Mackinac is short for Michilimackinac, which was an Indian territory on what is now Mackinac Island. Measured the conventional way, between towers, Mackinac Bridge is the third-longest suspension bridge in the United States. Measured by impact, it ranks right up there with the Golden Gate Bridge. No wonder Michiganders call it "Mighty Mac."

(Above) The nearly five-mile-long **Mackinac Bridge**, including approaches, links Michigan's upper and lower peninsulas.

(Below) There is enough beach for everyone at **Sleeping Bear Dunes National Lakeshore**. And that's just one of its attractions.

SLEEPING BEAR DUNES NATIONAL LAKESHORE

You'll find sand beaches, lush forests, clear inland lakes, picturesque farms, and bluffs that rise as high as 460 feet above Lake Michigan at Sleeping Bear Dunes National Lakeshore. While the dunes are a popular attraction in this protected area, the entire 35-mile stretch of Lake Michigan's eastern coastline, as well as North and South Manitou Islands, are worth a visit.

MICHIGAN PLACES TO VISIT
- Henry Ford Museum and Greenfield Village (Dearborn)
- Colonial Michilimackinac (Mackinaw City)
- Mackinac Island State Park (Mackinac Island)
- Gerald R. Ford Presidential Museum (Grand Rapids)
- Grand Rapids Art Museum (Grand Rapids)
- Windmill Island (Holland)

WISCONSIN

WISCONSIN PLACES TO VISIT
- Wisconsin State Capitol (Madison)
- Harley-Davidson Museum (Milwaukee)
- Circus World Museum (Baraboo)
- AirVenture Show and Museum (Oshkosh)
- National Railroad Museum (Green Bay)

LAMBEAU FIELD

Lambeau Field in Green Bay, Wisconsin, is one of those magical stadiums where the game experience evokes a rich past. Lambeau Field was built in 1957. It was named in 1965 for the Packers' great first coach, Earl L. "Curly" Lambeau, after his death. Vince Lombardi, head coach of the Packers from 1958 to 1967, was the first to coach the team in the new stadium. The stadium was renovated in 2003, but that hasn't diluted the Lambeau Field magic. It has been continuously occupied longer than any other stadium in the National Football League.

Pabst commissioned Milwaukee architect George Bowman Ferry to design the mansion in 1889. Construction was completed in 1892.

Despite Wisconsin's often-frigid weather, Packers fans cheer on their beloved football team with unmatched zeal.

CAPTAIN FREDERICK PABST MANSION

The Pabst Mansion in Milwaukee was the 1892 creation of Frederick Pabst, whose many titles included sea captain, beer baron, real estate mogul, philanthropist, and patron of the arts. The heavy, square architecture was patterned after the 16th-century palaces and fortresses in Flanders, Belgium. With 37 rooms, 12 baths, and 14 fireplaces, the mansion lives up to its name. In its time, the house was a high-tech marvel featuring electricity, plumbing for 9 bathrooms, and 16 thermostats. The foyer and massive wood-carved Grand Stair Hall are breathtaking. Today, Pabst Mansion is called "the Finest Flemish Renaissance Revival Mansion in America."

Door County (the long, finger-shape peninsula that separates the main body of Lake Michigan from the city of Green Bay) is known for its quiet beaches, picturesque towns, historic lighthouses, and scenic farms.

Taliesin is regarded as a prime example of Frank Lloyd Wright's organic architecture. The house is located in Spring Green, Wisconsin. On tours you'll see many structures Wright built on the 600-acre estate.

MILWAUKEE ART MUSEUM

In 1957, the Milwaukee Art Center opened its Eero Saarinen Building, named after the architect who designed it (he is also the acclaimed architect of the St. Louis Gateway Arch). The building has a floating cruciform shape with four large wings that cantilever in space. In 2001, the Quadracci Pavilion, designed by Santiago Calatrava, was added to the building. The pavilion has attracted worldwide attention for its light, lacy facade that curves like a sail, despite being built from concrete. The museum's collections include works by Degas, Homer, Monet, O'Keeffe, Picasso, Rodin, and Warhol.

The Quadracci Pavilion at the Milwaukee Art Museum was the first building designed by Santiago Calatrava to be completed in the United States.

MINNESOTA

VOYAGEURS NATIONAL PARK

Voyageurs National Park is the rare roadless national park. The park pays historic tribute to the Voyageurs, fur trappers, and traders required to work 14 or more hours per day, portage—carry over land—26-foot canoes with 180 pounds or more worth of goods, and sometimes paddle at a rate of almost one stroke per second. Today, the park's nearly 220,000 acres are accessible only by waterway; nonetheless about a quarter-million visitors come yearly.

More than 1,200 miles of canoe routes weave through the wilderness of the **Boundary Waters**.

BOUNDARY WATERS CANOE AREA WILDERNESS

The Boundary Waters Canoe Area Wilderness is the busiest wilderness area in the United States, drawing more than 200,000 visitors each year. The Boundary Waters stretch along almost 150 miles of the Canadian border in northeastern Minnesota. The region is a mass of marshes, lakes, and bogs on terrain once raked by glaciers at the edge of the Canadian Shield. Waterfalls plunge off cliffs, and you can catch a glimpse of native wildlife, such as otters, deer, moose, beavers, ducks, loons, osprey, and bald eagles. The wilderness is perfect for canoeing, fishing, and camping.

Vibrant sunsets over the tranquil lakes and bays of **Voyageurs** are stunning.

Watching ships pass under the iconic **Aerial Lift Bridge** in Canal Park is a must when visiting Duluth, Minnesota.

The 2,220-acre Split Rock Lighthouse State Park is located on the North Shore of Lake Superior. The park is known for the **Split Rock Lighthouse**, which was completed in 1910.

MINNEAPOLIS SCULPTURE GARDEN

Since opening in 1988, the Minneapolis Sculpture Garden has welcomed millions of visitors, showcasing more than 40 works from the Walker Art Center's collections, including the famous "Spoonbridge and Cherry." After touring the Garden, take a stroll over to the Walker Art Center. It is one of the most-visited modern and contemporary art museums in the U.S.

"Spoonbridge and Cherry" has become a beloved icon at the **Minneapolis Sculpture Garden**. Claes Oldenburg and Coosje van Bruggen designed it.

IOWA

AMANA COLONIES

The Amana Colonies made up a historic utopian society in the gently rolling hills of Iowa's River Valley. Established shortly before the Civil War by German immigrants of the Community of True Inspiration sect, the colonies today are on the National Park Service National Register of Historic Places. The Amana communities encompass 20,000 acres and 31 historic places. They were one of the world's longest active communal societies, lasting from 1855 to 1932. Almost 500 buildings once part of the communities have survived. Visitors can start at the Museum of Amana History, which helps explain what the communities' religionists called "the Great Change" away from shared life.

Almost 500 original buildings have survived, including the **Amana Furniture Shop**.

PLACES TO VISIT IN IOWA

- Effigy Mounds National Monument (Harpers Ferry)
- National Mississippi River Museum and Aquarium (Dubuque)
- National Czech & Slovak Museum and Library (Cedar Rapids)
- Iowa State Capitol (Des Moines)
- Des Moines Art Center (Des Moines)
- Herbert Hoover National Historic Site (West Branch)
- American Gothic House (Eldon)
- Buffalo Bill Museum (LeClaire)
- Adventureland (Altoon)

The Holliwell Bridge is one of the six original bridges still standing in Madison County.

BRIDGES OF MADISON COUNTY

Madison County, Iowa, used to be a typical Midwestern farm area. The county was notable as the birthplace of John Wayne, for the home of the 18-acre Madison County Historical Society building, and for its rustic covered bridges. Then Robert James Waller wrote the best-selling novel, *The Bridges of Madison County*. Today, Madison County's covered bridges have become such a tourist draw that the county now is building reproductions of lost covered bridges. Madison County at one time tallied 19 picturesque covered bridges; today just six of the original bridges survive, and five are on the National Register of Historic Places.

The Vermeer Mill in Pella, Iowa, reaches a height of 124 feet and 6 inches, making it the tallest working windmill in the U.S.

The Grotto of Redemption in West Bend, Iowa, is comprised of nine separate grottos, each portraying a scene in the life of Jesus.

IOWA STATE FAIR

When it comes to state fairs, Iowa brings home the blue ribbon. It has more competitive events than any other state fair in the nation. You'll find concerts featuring chart-topping performers, acres of farm equipment, one of the world's largest livestock shows, and agricultural displays of all types. The food ranges from fair favorites such as funnel cakes, corn dogs, and cotton candy to chocolate-covered cheesecake on a stick, sweet potato fries, and fried ice cream.

You can explore the many rides and games on the **Iowa State Fair**'s expansive midway.

MISSOURI

GATEWAY ARCH NATIONAL PARK

Gateway Arch National Park, formerly known as the Jefferson National Expansion Memorial, is a park in St. Louis, Missouri, near the starting point of the Lewis and Clark Expedition. The park is a memorial to Thomas Jefferson's role in opening the West, to the pioneers who shaped its history, and to Dred Scott who sued for his freedom in the Old Courthouse. The country's tallest man-made memorial and the site of several significant court decisions make the park a must-see destination.

The Old Courthouse, the oldest standing building in downtown St. Louis, is now the visitors' center for Gateway Arch National Park. The Courthouse was the site of the first two trials of the pivotal Dred Scott case in 1847 and 1850. It was also where Virginia Minor's case for a woman's right to vote came to trial in the 1870s.

At 630 feet tall, the **Gateway Arch** is the nation's tallest monument. The arch was designed by Finnish-American architect Eero Saarinen in 1947 and completed in 1965. The top of the arch is accessible by two trams—one in each leg—that are made up of eight cylindrical, five-seat compartments.

Meramec Caverns is a cavern system in the Ozarks, near Stanton, Missouri. According to local legend, outlaw Jesse James once used the tunnels as a hideout.

PLACES TO VISIT IN MISSOURI

- Harry S. Truman National Historic Site (Independence)
- Wilson's Creek National Battlefield (Republic)
- George Washington Carver National Monument (Diamond)
- Missouri State Capitol (Jefferson City)
- Ulysses S. Grant National Historic Site (St. Louis)
- St. Louis Zoo (St. Louis)
- The Magic House (St. Louis)
- Kaleidoscope (Kansas City)
- Nelson-Atkins Museum of Art (Kansas City)
- Branson Strip (Branson)

Mark Twain National Forest encompasses 1.5 million acres of public land in 29 counties in Missouri. It contains several wilderness areas, natural areas, and the Eleven Point National Wild and Scenic River.

Ozark National Scenic Riverways is the first national park area to protect a river system. The park, which runs through Van Buren, Eminence, Salem, and Winona, Missouri, is home to hundreds of freshwater springs, caves, trails, and historic sites such as Alley Mill.

KANSAS

DODGE CITY

The lawless, gun-slinging reputation of this Kansas frontier town was well deserved. Beginning in the 1860s, Dodge City drew all sorts of people who traveled along the Santa Fe Trail (and later the Atchison, Topeka, and Santa Fe Railroad). Gambling and prostitution ran rampant, and the term "red light district" was coined here after the train masters who would take their red caboose lanterns out with them. With no law in town, disagreements often led to sudden death.

Today Dodge City celebrates its past. Recreations of Front Street, the Long Branch Saloon, and Boot Hill Cemetery are a reminder of the Old West and its colorful history. There are also tours of Fort Dodge and the Mueller-Schmidt House Museum (the oldest house in Dodge City).

The notorious Front Street of 1876, the business district of Old Dodge City, has been recreated as a tourist attraction.

A "Ring of Fire" surrounds the statue—fire pits that are lit for a period at night as the weather permits.

KEEPER OF THE PLAINS

At the place where the Arkansas and Little Arkansas rivers meet, a 44-foot-tall statue stands proudly atop a 30-foot pedestal. Called *The Keeper of the Plains* and designed by Kiowa-Comanche sculptor Blackbear Bosin, the statue depicts an American Indian chief. It was commissioned to celebrate the United States Bicentennial and erected in 1974.

PLACES TO VISIT IN KANSAS

- Fort Larned National Historic Site (Larned)
- Eisenhower Presidential Library and Museum (Abilene)
- Deanna Rose Children's Farmstead (Overland Park)
- Brown v. Board of Education National Historic Site (Topeka)
- Kansas State Capitol (Topeka)
- Evel Knievel Museum (Topeka)
- Safari Zoological Park (Caney)
- Fort Scott National Historic Site (Fort Scott)
- Botanica, Wichita Gardens (Wichita)

Monument Rocks (also called Chalk Pyramids) are a series of large chalk formations in Gove County. The chalk formations include buttes and arches.

TALLGRASS PRAIRIE NATIONAL PRESERVE

Of the 170 million acres of tallgrass prairie that once covered North America, less than 4 percent remains today, mostly in the Flint Hills of Kansas. The Tallgrass Prairie National Preserve protects nearly 11,000 acres of the once vast tallgrass prairie.

Between 30 and 60 million bison once roamed North America. By 1890, less than 1,000 remained. The **Tallgrass Prairie National Preserve** is now home to a growing bison herd.

NEBRASKA

CHIMNEY ROCK

Chimney Rock rises to a spire almost 325 feet above the North Platte River Valley in Nebraska. It can be seen from miles away, so it was the ideal landmark for pioneers traveling the Mormon, California, and Oregon trails. Today, Chimney Rock is a National Historic Site that still marks the place where the plains give way to the Rocky Mountains.

Scotts Bluff National Monument is another site in Nebraska related to the Oregon Trail. The natural geological formations acted as landmarks to travelers.

Chimney Rock is a distinct formation that can still be seen along the historic Oregon Trail.

SCOTTS BLUFF NATIONAL MONUMENT

About 45 minutes from Chimney Rock is Scotts Bluff National Monument, another important three-trail landmark. The monument is striking for its key features—Scotts Bluff and South Bluff and their dramatic cliffs. The monument also boasts barren badlands between Scotts Bluff and the North Platte River, providing a smorgasbord of landscapes in its 3,000 acres. A museum on the national monument grounds houses exhibits about the area's history.

CARHENGE

In the small town of Alliance, Nebraska, is the unusual sculpture known as Carhenge. Carhenge is a replica of Stonehenge in terms of size and orientation, but the story of its origin is a bit different.

As creator Jim Reinders explained, it was just "something to do at our family reunion." Reinders wasn't kidding: Carhenge was built during a reunion at the family farm in 1987. Reinders and 35 of his relatives grabbed their backhoes, found a forklift, and worked seven 8-hour days to position the 38 cars, which were painted battleship gray in accordance with Stonehenge's appearance. People were immediately drawn to Carhenge, despite its rather remote location. An estimated 40,000 to 80,000 folks visit each year.

Jim Reinders and his family arranged old cars to make **Carhenge** matching the configuration of Stonehenge.

Beneath the Desert Dome at the **Henry Doorly Zoo and Aquarium** in Omaha, Nebraska, you'll find Kingdoms of the Night. The exhibit covers 42,000 square feet and is home to 75 animals.

PLACES TO VISIT IN NEBRASKA

- Holy Family Shrine (Gretna)
- Old Market (Omaha)
- Omaha Children's Museum (Omaha)
- Bob Kerrey Pedestrian Bridge (Omaha)
- Henry Doorly Zoo and Aquarium (Omaha)
- Strategic Air and Space Museum (Ashland)
- Haymarket District (Lincoln)
- Golden Spike Tower (North Platte)
- Great Platte River Road Archway (Kearney)

SOUTH DAKOTA

Rapid erosion of the plateaus of soft sediment and volcanic ash etched the Dakota Badlands.

BADLANDS NATIONAL PARK

Badlands National Park in southwestern South Dakota is 244,000 acres of buttes, pinnacles, and spires. Strange shapes carved into soft sedimentary rock and volcanic ash dot the landscape of the park. Because the land is so dry, wind and water cause rapid erosion of the sprawling rock formations. The result is a rugged terrain unlike any other in the United States. Badlands is divided into two separate sections of four units. The most visited unit is the Cedar Pass Area, near Interior, South Dakota. Try to visit the Badlands Wilderness Area Sage Creek Unit, a primitive camping area, as well.

MOUNT RUSHMORE

This presidential face-off of monumental proportions is a jaw-dropping feat of art and engineering. Blasted and chiseled out of granite, Mount Rushmore features four presidents: George Washington, Thomas Jefferson, Theodore Roosevelt, and Abraham Lincoln. The faces on the 5,725-foot-tall landmark tower over a majestic forest of pine, spruce, birch, and aspen trees in South Dakota's Black Hills. Sculptor Gutzon Borglum and his team carved the four 60-foot-high faces into the rock between 1927 and 1941. Today, Mount Rushmore National Memorial is South Dakota's most popular tourist attraction.

George Washington, Thomas Jefferson, Theodore Roosevelt, and Abraham Lincoln gaze over South Dakota.

SOUTH DAKOTA PLACES TO VISIT

- Wind Cave National Park (Hot Springs)
- Mammoth Site (Hot Springs)
- Spearfish Canyon (near Spearfish)
- Jewel Cave National Monument (Custer)
- National Music Museum (Vermillion)
- Good Earth State Park (near Sioux Falls)
- Blood Run National Historic Landmark (near Sioux Falls)
- Butterfly House & Aquarium (Sioux Falls)
- Old Courthouse Museum (Sioux Falls)

Deadwood, South Dakota, is a National Historic Landmark District with well-preserved Gold Rush-era architecture.

Custer State Park in southwestern South Dakota contains one of the nation's largest free roaming bison herds. The park is also home to bighorn sheep, antelope, deer, elk, coyote, and prairie dogs.

When the **Crazy Horse Memorial** near Rapid City is completed, it will be taller than the Washington Monument and larger than the Sphinx in Egypt.

NORTH DAKOTA

This rugged landscape inspired Theodore Roosevelt's conservationist drive.

THEODORE ROOSEVELT NATIONAL PARK

Part of the expansive North Dakota badlands, Theodore Roosevelt National Park commemorates the conservation policies of the 26th U.S. president. The park covers more than 70,000 acres, of which 30,000 are wilderness. It's divided into three units: The South Unit (the most-visited area), Elkhorn Ranch (Theodore Roosevelt's ranch), and the North Unit (near the headwaters of the Little Missouri River). If you hike or ride horseback through the park, you can spend days out of sight of civilization. Take a leisurely drive, and stop at the overlooks to view the ragged landscape or tour the restored cow town of Medora. Or, hike the half-mile Wind Canyon Trail to see a remarkable view of the strangely beautiful badlands and the Little Missouri River.

NORTH DAKOTA STATE CAPITOL

The North Dakota State Capitol, a 19-story building known as "The Skyscraper on the Prairie," towers over Bismarck. While the capitol stands only 241 feet and 8 inches tall, in winter, its upper stories often disappear in low-hanging clouds. The capitol complex and grounds have become the site for many memorials and museums, including the North Dakota State Heritage Center Museum and Fountain Garden, the Pioneer Family Statue, the Statue of Sakajawea, and the North Dakota Hall of Fame. Guided tours of the building, including a visit to the 18th-floor observation deck, are also available.

This Art Deco skyscraper replaced the original state capitol, which burned down in 1930.

FORT ABRAHAM LINCOLN

A trip to this picturesque frontier fort and state park on the upper Missouri River will take you back to another century, to the time when this fort was the largest and most important on the Northern Plains. It was from this fort that General George A. Custer and the Seventh Cavalry rode off to meet their destiny at Little Bighorn.

Visitors to **Fort Abraham Lincoln** are invited into the home of General George Custer (above), appointed exactly as it was in 1875.

The Enchanted Highway, in Regent, North Dakota, is a series of large metal sculptures by Gary Greff along 32-mile stretch of highway. *Pheasants on the Prairie* (above) was added in 1996.

The International Peace Garden consists of more than 150,000 flowers, planted annually and shaped into a dramatically beautiful landscape among trees and fountains.

INTERNATIONAL PEACE GARDEN

The International Peace Garden spans the invisible line where North Dakota becomes Manitoba. Officials from the United States and Canada dedicated the garden in 1932. The monuments to peace include girders from the World Trade Center and seven "Peace Poles"—gifts from Japan inscribed with "May Peace Prevail" in 28 languages. Another notable feature of the International Peace Garden is the floral clock. The clock is 18 feet in diameter and displays 2,000 to 5,000 plants, depending on the type of plant and the design on the face of the clock.

NORTH DAKOTA PLACES TO VISIT
- National Buffalo Museum (Jamestown)
- Knife River Indian Villages National Historic Site (Stanton)
- North Dakota Heritage Center (Bismarck)
- Plains Art Museum (Fargo)
- Fort Mandan (Washburn)

TEXAS

THE ALAMO

The Alamo is Texas's most visited site. The architecture of this historic mission church, now surrounded by modern downtown San Antonio, is hard to forget.

Spanish missionaries established the Mission San Antonio de Valero in the vicinity of the Alamo in 1718 and worked to convert the local people to Catholicism. They began building the Alamo in 1724 after a hurricane decimated the original site. The Spanish secularized the mission in 1793. However, it was abandoned before the legendary battle of 1836 broke out.

The missionaries' onetime living quarters, the Long Barrack, have been turned into a museum that recounts Texas's turbulent past, emphasizing the memorable two-week Battle of the Alamo. Also onsite are the serene Alamo Gardens, which provide a good spot to rest and reflect.

The Alamo remains an icon and reminder of Texas's struggle for independence.

PLACES TO VISIT IN TEXAS

- Presidio County Courthouse (Marfa)
- Amistad National Recreation Area (Del Rio)
- Natural Bridge Caverns (San Antonio)
- Waco Mammoth (Waco)
- Texas State Capitol (Austin)
- Stockyards National Historic District (Fort Worth)
- USS *Lexington* (Corpus Christi)
- Sixth Floor Museum (Dallas)
- Houston Livestock Show and Rodeo (Houston)

San Antonio's lively downtown area is known for its **Riverwalk**, a tree-lined, flower-filled oasis of cool walkways, shops, and cafés located along the river.

THE RIVERWALK

The popular Riverwalk, also known as Paseo del Rio, forms a vibrant circle around downtown San Antonio, Texas, along the San Antonio River. After the 1968 HemisFair exposition in San Antonio, commercial development along the Riverwalk boomed, and hotels, galleries, restaurants, and boutiques now crowd the river's banks. Visitors can take narrated tours along the river, which last about 35 to 40 minutes and are available daily.

BIG BEND NATIONAL PARK

Big Bend National Park is named for the turn of the Rio Grande along the park's southern boundary in southwest Texas. Winding through Big Bend, the Rio Grande has carved three of the continent's most striking canyons—Boquillas, Mariscal, and Santa Elena. Rafters are drawn to the waterway, and hikers climb trails winding through the mountains, with the desert acting as a gateway to the north. Surrounded by beautiful, gnarled desert, the heart of Big Bend is the Chisos Mountain Range. Cloaked in green forest, the lush mountains are a sharp contrast to the arid surroundings.

(Left) The chasms chiseled by the Rio Grande draw adventurous rafters to explore **Big Bend National Park**.

SPACE CENTER HOUSTON

As the official visitor center for NASA's Johnson Space Center, Space Center Houston gives visitors an in-depth look at the United States' space program. The Space Center Houston has exhibits including the Kids Space Place and the Astronaut and Starship galleries. The giant-screen theater shows films on space exploration, and interactive simulators allow lay people to get a feel for space travel. The fascinating behind-the-scenes tram tour is the best way to observe the nuts and bolts of NASA. The tram makes stops at hangars throughout the operational Johnson Space Center, historic Johnson Mission Control, and the International Space Station Assembly Building.

(Right) Pete Conrad's spacesuit from the Apollo 12 mission to the moon is part of the Astronaut Gallery at **Space Center Houston**.

AUSTIN

Austin stands out from most Texan metropolises. Austin has a Bohemian aura, due in part to the University of Texas campus. The aroma of barbecue and Tex-Mex cuisine hangs in the air, and the nightclub-lined Sixth Street is one of the best spots for live music in the entire world. And politics prevail here: Austin is Texas's capital city, and its capitol building is the largest in the country.

There are 1.5 million Mexican free-tailed bats that hang from downtown Austin's **Congress Avenue Bridge**, which spans the Colorado River. Crowds gather to watch them emerge en masse at sunset.

Rising 8,085 feet above sea level, the impressive **El Capitán** soars over the rugged landscape of Guadalupe Mountains National Park.

GUADALUPE MOUNTAINS NATIONAL PARK

At the tip of the Trans-Pecos region (the far west Texas panhandle), the Guadalupe Mountains loom over the surroundings like mighty centurions. The rocky cliffs developed long ago when today's desert was an ancient ocean. The summit of Guadalupe Peak (8,749 feet above sea level) offers sublime views of the surrounding desert. McKittrick Canyon, believed by many to be the prettiest spot in the state, is a vestige of the last ice age that explodes with color in the fall.

BIG THICKET NATIONAL PRESERVE

East Texas's 97,000-acre Big Thicket National Preserve is where the sultry swamps of the South, the verdant forests of the East, and the seemingly endless savannah of the Great Plains meet and mingle. Meadows are scarce. In Big Thicket's diverse biosphere, desert roadrunners live alongside swamp critters, such as alligators and frogs. And they coexist near deer, mountain lions, and 300 species of nesting and migratory birds. This is the only place on the planet where many of these species live side by side.

Big Thicket National Preserve provides a unique habitat of rich wetlands and thick forests that harbors diverse plant life.

PADRE ISLAND NATIONAL SEASHORE

The pristine beaches, wind-sculpted dunes, and saltwater marshes of Padre Island National Seashore stretch for 80 miles along the Gulf of Mexico off of south Texas. Padre Island's major migratory bird flyway makes it ideal for bird-watching. Padre Island also offers speckled trout, black drum, redfish, and flounder for fishing enthusiasts. The saltwater lagoon between the island and the mainland is a perfect place to learn to windsurf. Pack a picnic, and watch one of the world-class windsurfing competitions held throughout the year.

The park is a safe nesting ground for the Kemp's ridley sea turtle.

NEW MEXICO MISSIONS

In 1598, Spanish conquistador Don Juan de Oñate crossed the Rio Grande near modern-day El Paso, Texas. De Oñate led his party north past Franciscan missionaries along the Rio Grande's banks to its intersection with the Chama River. Here he established the San Gabriel Mission, New Mexico's second Spanish capital, in 1600—a full seven years before the English settled in Jamestown, Virginia.

In 1610, the Spanish capital moved to Santa Fe, where San Miguel Mission, now considered the oldest operational church in the United States, was established. Another nicely preserved church from this early era is the Mission of San José at Laguna Pueblo (1699), 45 miles west of Albuquerque. About 25 miles to the southwest is the Mission of San Esteban del Rey at Acoma Pueblo, perched majestically on a 367-foot sandstone mesa. To the southeast are the ruins of four more 17th-century missions that were abandoned before 1700 and now comprise Salinas Pueblo Missions National Monument.

NEW MEXICO

TAOS PUEBLO

The Taos Pueblo in northern New Mexico is the oldest continuously occupied structure on the continent. Dating back to A.D. 1000, its adobe walls today house about 150 Taos Native Americans who maintain the ancient traditions of their ancestors. The Pueblo consists of two long, multistory adobe structures, one on each side of a freshwater creek. You can explore on your own, or take an escorted tour that recounts the Pueblo's history, which includes occupation by Spanish conquistadors in 1540 and by Franciscan friars in the 1590s.

(Left) **San Esteban del Rey** was the mission built from 1629 to 1640 at Acoma Pueblo.

(Below) **Taos Pueblo** is made from adobe—a mix of sun-dried earth and straw.

ROSWELL

On July 4, 1947, many residents of Roswell, New Mexico, reported seeing an unidentified flying object streaking across the night sky. Other locals reported a loud explosion. The next week, the local newspaper, the *Roswell Daily Record,* reported that the authorities at Roswell Army Air Field had found the remains of a flying saucer that crash-landed in the vicinity. However, officials recanted the initial account within days and said it was a weather-balloon experiment gone awry. So, did the government cover up a UFO crash and take the wreckage to the now infamous Area 51, or was the object really a weather balloon? Visitors flock to Roswell's International UFO Museum to judge for themselves.

The International UFO Museum and Research Center at Roswell is dedicated to collecting and preserving materials and information relevant to the 1947 Roswell incident and other unexplained phenomena.

The vast **Big Room** at Carlsbad Caverns has a ceiling that arches 255 feet above the floor, and it contains a six-story stalagmite and the so-called bottomless pit, which is more than 700 feet deep.

CARLSBAD CAVERNS NATIONAL PARK

This enormous cave system was created by water dripping through an ancient reef made of porous limestone. More than 30 miles of the main cavern have been explored, and the three miles of caves that are open to visitors are among the largest and most magnificent underground formations in the world. In the summer months, bats that inhabit parts of the caverns are an additional attraction. Each evening at sunset the creatures swarm out of the cave. The event is best observed at the Bat Flight Amphitheater at the cavern entrance.

NEW MEXICO PLACES TO VISIT

- White Sands National Monument (Alamogordo)
- Bandelier National Monument (Los Alamos)
- Chaco Culture National Historical Park (Nageezi)
- Cumbres & Toltec Scenic Railroad (Chama)
- Gila Cliff Dwellings National Monument (Silver City)
- Billy the Kid Museum (Fort Sumner)
- Pecos National Historical Park (Pecos)
- Petroglyph National Monument (Albuquerque)

SANTA FE PLAZA

The Santa Fe Plaza has been a bustling outdoor market since the early 1600s. The Plaza is lined with shade trees, famous landmarks, and museums, including the Palace of the Governors. Native American artisans display their wares on beautiful blankets in front of the Palace: You'll see silver-and-turquoise jewelry, pottery, leatherwork, and hand-woven blankets for sale. The central area is open, and what once was used for town meetings and livestock grazing is now ideal for people-watching.

(Left and below) Dominating the north side of the Santa Fe Plaza is the **Palace of the Governors**, where local artisans display their wares.

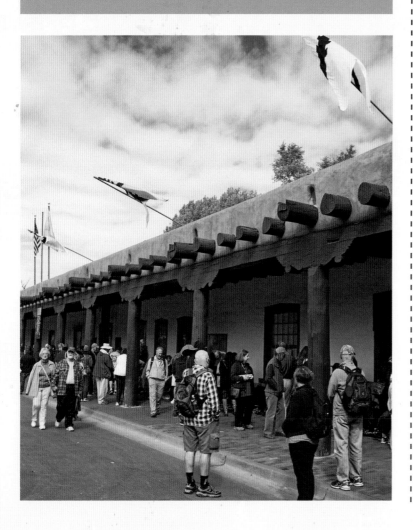

ARIZONA

GRAND CANYON NATIONAL PARK

Millions of years of erosion caused by wind and the Colorado River have carved and sculpted Arizona's Grand Canyon, truly one of the world's most dramatic natural wonders. At 227 miles long and 18 miles across at its widest point, this breathtaking abyss plunges more than a mile from rim to river bottom at its deepest point.

The South Rim area attracts roughly 90 percent of the park's visitors, largely because the views are thought to be better and it has the majority of the park's accommodations and restaurants. Stroll along the paved South Rim Trail, or exercise your legs on the steep switchbacks of Bright Angel Trail to get a real view of the landscape. Visitors seeking tranquility should head to the less-visited North Rim. It has lodge accommodations, hiking trails, camping, and somewhat limited services.

The Grand Canyon Skywalk is a horseshoe-shape, glass-bottom walkway that extends over the edge of the canyon and gives visitors the opportunity to look 4,000 feet straight down.

Wind and water eroded the canyon's rocky landscape, revealing colorful layers of limestone, sandstone, and shale.

PETRIFIED FOREST

Some 225 million years ago, the arid desert of north-central Arizona was a lush tropical forest dominated by towering conifers. This era ended when catastrophic floods devastated the area, uprooting trees. Over millions of years, layers of silt, mud, and volcanic ash covered the spent trees and slowed the process of decay. Silica from the ash gradually penetrated the wood and turned to quartz. Minerals streaked the former wood with every color of the rainbow. Beyond the magnificent petrified wood, Petrified Forest National Park also contains one of the best fossil records from the Late Triassic period.

The view of **Cathedral Rock** from Red Rock Crossing is unforgettable.

SEDONA

At the base of the Mogollon Rim and its lofty formations of vibrant red sandstone lies Sedona, Arizona. Atop the Mogollon Rim, many of the wondrous sandstone formations that tower over Sedona are named after objects they appear to mimic, such as Cathedral Rock, Coffeepot Rock, and even Snoopy Rock, named for the character from the comic strip Peanuts. Boutiques and art galleries are common along the town's cobblestone roads, and visitors enjoy intimate restaurants, friendly local cafés, and quaint bed-and-breakfasts.

Over millions of years, ancient trees in Arizona were streaked with minerals and preserved as shimmering petrified wood.

TALIESIN WEST

In the late 1930s, Frank Lloyd Wright designed and built the Taliesin West complex in Scottsdale, Arizona, as the winter counterpart to his original Taliesin in Spring Green, Wisconsin. Taliesin West covers 600 acres of rugged Sonoran Desert at the foot of McDowell Mountain. The landscape is an integral part of the site: Wright employed rocks and sand on the property as key ingredients in his masterpiece.

(Right) The organic design of **Taliesin West** blends perfectly with the surrounding arid landscape.

CANYON DE CHELLY

Canyon de Chelly in northeastern Arizona blends archaeology, history, and geology. The canyon was carved by eons of runoff from spring storms and has been inhabited by humans for about 2,000 years. The cliff dwellings are spectacular structures with perfectly preserved specimens and ruins set in deep caves at the base of vivid red and yellow sandstone walls. An incredible vista of cottonwood trees, green pastures, and fields of maize surround the caves.

(Right) The red sandstone monolith **Spider Rock** towers 800 feet above the floor of Canyon de Chelly.

ARIZONA PLACES TO VISIT

- Monument Valley (Arizona-Utah border)
- Glen Canyon National Recreation Area (Arizona and Utah)
- Saguaro National Park (Tucson)
- Sabino Canyon (Tucson)
- Antelope Canyon (near Page)
- Organ Pipe Cactus National Monument (Ajo)
- Tumacácori National Historical Park (Tumacácori)
- Lake Mead National Recreation Area (Mojave Desert)
- Montezuma Castle National Monument (Camp Verde)

WINDOW ROCK

Window Rock is both a community and a geological masterstroke. It is the capital of the Navajo Nation, the largest Native American government in the United States, and home to about 3,000 people. Window Rock is also a natural landmark—the city took its name from the wondrous pothole arch.

Over millions of years, sunlight, wind, water, and chemical exfoliation formed the distinctive window. These elements slowly peeled away layer after layer of red sandstone, leaving a nearly perfect circular hole in its place. The formation is known as *Tséghahoodzání*, which in Navajo means "Perforated Rock."

(Above) Chemical and thermal exfoliation of Entrada sandstone created the astonishing arch known as **Window Rock**.

NEVADA

LAS VEGAS STRIP

The Strip (Las Vegas Boulevard) dwarfs the downtown area when the cityscape first comes into view. Eleven of the 20 largest hotels in the world are on this four-mile slice of real estate in the middle of the Nevada desert. A visitor walking the Strip could see everything from replicas of the Eiffel Tower and the New York skyline to dazzling water fountains that dance to music. Big-name performers take to the stages here nightly, entertaining the vacationing masses with comedy, magic, music, and dance. While casinos still dominate the resorts, the Strip has grown increasingly diverse, cultured, and family-friendly over the years.

The ornate palaces of **South Las Vegas Boulevard** and their endless ribbons of neon make it one of the few stretches of road that's more scenic at night.

Nevada's second-tallest mountain, **Wheeler Peak**, reaches an elevation of 13,063 feet in Great Basin National Park.

GREAT BASIN NATIONAL PARK

Amidst the lonely desert that unfolds between the Rockies and the Sierras, a rugged landscape rises into the beautiful blue sky of eastern Nevada. Forested mountains tower a mile above the flatlands below. Great Basin, which was cut by glaciers, has been a national park since 1986 and is defined by the Snake Range, which has 13 peaks that rise more than 11,000 feet high and nearly 100 valleys snaking among the soaring summits. Alpine lakes cascade into rollicking streams and rivers, and the bristlecone pine forest opens into lush meadows dotted with wildflowers.

PYRAMID LAKE

Named for the distinctive 400-foot rock near its eastern shore, Pyramid Lake is a striking contrast to its rugged, arid surroundings in northwestern Nevada. The lake is one of the largest desert lakes in the world and is famous for its tufa rock formations. Located on the Paiute Indian Reservation, Pyramid Lake's warm, shallow waters are a magnet for anglers and swimmers.

NEVADA PLACES TO VISIT

- Lake Tahoe (Nevada-California border)
- Valley of Fire State Park (Clark County)
- Lake Mead National Recreation Area (Mojave Desert)
- Red Rock Canyon National Conservation Area (near Las Vegas)
- Tule Springs Fossil Beds National Monument (Las Vegas)
- Burning Man (Black Rock Desert)
- Lamoille Canyon (Elko County)

The Hoover Dam is a National Historic Landmark and has been selected by the American Society of Civil Engineers as one of "America's Seven Modern Civil Engineering Wonders."

HOOVER DAM

In the Black Canyon of the Colorado River, 30 miles southeast of Las Vegas, sits the engineering marvel known as Hoover Dam. The dam was constructed between 1931 and 1935 and consists of 3.25 million cubic yards of concrete. The dam widens the Colorado into the vast waters of Lake Mead, a year-round recreation destination that attracts millions of visitors each year for swimming, boating, waterskiing, and fishing.

OKLAHOMA

OKLAHOMA CITY NATIONAL MEMORIAL

At this peaceful plaza in downtown Oklahoma City, the east gate is inscribed with the time 9:01, the west gate with 9:03. The first time represents the moment innocence was lost; the second one the time healing began. On the morning of April 19, 1995, a terrorist's bomb took the lives of 168 people at the Alfred P. Murrah Federal Building in this southwestern city.

The stark gates frame 168 forever-empty chairs, representing the lives lost that tragic morning. The chairs surround a single American elm, the Survivor Tree. The site is a stirring, visceral reminder of the damage done by violence and the resilience of the human spirit.

Designers Hans and Torrey Butzer created the concept for the memorial chairs honoring the 168 people who were killed.

NATIONAL COWBOY & WESTERN HERITAGE MUSEUM

The National Cowboy & Western Heritage Museum in Oklahoma City has a pretty broad mission statement: "To preserve and interpret the heritage of the American West for the enrichment of the public." But that all-encompassing spirit has led to the development of a world-class, 200,000-square-foot complex showcasing one of the United States' top collections of Western art, with works by such legends as Charles Russell and Albert Bierstadt. "Canyon Princess" is one of the famous sculptures on display at the museum. The 16,000-pound white marble cougar by sculptor Gerald Balciar guards the entrance to the Gaylord Exhibition Wing.

This statue of Buffalo Bill sits outside the **National Cowboy & Western Heritage Museum**.

Guides help visitors to the **Marland Mansion** uncover the story of E.W. Marland's adopted daughter, Lydie, who became his second wife. This statue of Lydie Marland is found on the estate grounds.

OKLAHOMA PLACES TO VISIT
- Woody Guthrie Folk Festival (Okemah)
- Chickasaw National Recreation Area (Sulphur)
- Myriad Botanical Gardens (Oklahoma City)
- Museum of the Great Plains (Lawton)
- Woolaroc Museum & Wildlife Preserve (Bartlesville)
- Cherokee Heritage Center (Park Hill)
- Oklahoma Route 66 Museum (Clinton)
- Philbrook Museum of Art (Tulsa)
- Gilcrease Museum (Tulsa)
- Stafford Air & Space Museum (Weatherford)

The Marland Mansion has 55 rooms, including 10 bedrooms, 12 bathrooms, and 3 kitchens, plus expansive grounds with a swimming pool, artist studio, and boathouse.

MARLAND MANSION
The Marland Mansion in Ponca City, Oklahoma, was built between 1925 and 1928 by oil baron E.W. Marland. The 43,561-square-foot home is known as the "Palace on the Prairie." The palatial home was designated a National Historic Landmark in 1973, and is now open to the public.

COLORADO

MESA VERDE NATIONAL PARK

About 700 years ago, people now called the Anasazi lived in communities clinging to the cliffsides of the American Southwest. The name Anasazi originally meant "enemy ancestors" in Navajo but has come to mean "ancient people" or "ancient ones." These ancient people were the ancestors of today's Pueblo Indians, about 20 tribes including the Hopi and Zuni. They left a most remarkable legacy in what is now Mesa Verde ("green table" in Spanish) National Park, which comprises more than 4,000 archeological sites, including 600 cliff dwellings, in southwest Colorado.

Visitors can see a handful of the most spectacular of these uncanny ruins on tours led by park rangers, and trails to mesa tops are open to hikers. Some tourists balk at the regimentation of the guided tours, but regulation is the price today's travelers pay for the damage done by visitors before them.

Despite modern amenities, visitors should make no mistake that the park is part of the rugged American West. Hiking at an altitude of 8,400 feet with little humidity is a great way to enjoy Mesa Verde—just be sure to include lots of water, sunblock, and your best hiking boots.

ROCKY MOUNTAIN NATIONAL PARK

Perched atop the Continental Divide, Colorado's Rocky Mountain National Park is archetypal high country, offering a jaw-dropping panorama of daunting summits and alpine tundra in the mountains of north-central Colorado. Within the park are 78 peaks greater than 12,000 feet tall; 20 of them reach above 13,000 feet. Contrasting with this jagged terrain, meadows come alive in spring and summer as wildflowers poke their way through the tundra.

More than three million people visit the park each year. The drive along Trail Ridge Road from Estes Park on the east side to Grand Lake, its western gateway, reveals picturesque scenes. The park's bountiful backcountry is a world-class destination for climbing, fishing, hiking, and cross-country skiing. Estes Park features an abundance of family activities. A number of horseback-riding stables offer trail rides, and a small lake comes complete with boating and fishing. Other activities include bicycling and cultural events.

Crystalline lakes refilled by annual snowmelt are nestled at the feet of **Rocky Mountain National Park**'s awe-inspiring peaks.

(Left) The nicely shaded cliff dwellings in **Mesa Verde National Park** were home to the Anasazi people, who abandoned them about 700 years ago.

RED ROCKS PARK AND AMPHITHEATRE

In Morrison, Colorado, Red Rocks Park and Amphitheatre is nestled in the stunning mountainside and natural red rocks. Its acoustics are superb, perhaps rivaled only by the beauty of its spectacular surroundings. The north and south sides of the amphitheatre are 300-foot geological masterstrokes named Creation Rock and Ship Rock, respectively. The seats stretch across the steep slope between the two.

The dramatic red rock formations that give the **Red Rocks Amphitheatre** its name are both visually striking and acoustically ideal.

The snow-capped majesty of **Pikes Peak** looms over the red rock formations of Garden of Gods in Colorado Springs.

PIKES PEAK

Lieutenant Zebulon Pike first spied this 14,110-foot mountain along Colorado's Front Range in November 1806. But his attempt to scale the mountain that now bears his name was foiled by heavy snow. Pike said the rocky pinnacle would never be reached. But in 1820, Major Stephen Long led a party that reached the top of Pikes Peak in two days.

TELLURIDE

This picture-perfect Western boomtown on Colorado's Western Slope is nestled in a snug box canyon, surrounded by forested peaks and idyllic waterfalls. Telluride's beginning years in the late 1800s were marked by ambition. The silver veins in the surrounding mountains proved exceptionally rich. But Telluride's mining economy faltered after World War I, beginning a long, slow decline. But in 1972, the Telluride Ski Resort was born, and the population of miners gave way to Bohemians. The town's destiny changed suddenly. The entire town has been a National Landmark Historic District since 1964, and this status has kept its lovely character intact.

(Left) Tucked among the snow-capped Rockies, **Telluride** is a skier's paradise.

GREAT SAND DUNES NATIONAL PARK AND PRESERVE

Stretching across 8,000 square miles at an average elevation of 7,500 feet, southwestern Colorado's vast San Luis Valley is the world's largest alpine valley. It's full of mysteries and surprises, the most incredible of which may be the Great Sand Dunes, which have been continuously sculpted by wind, water, and time. In the shadow of the Sangre de Cristo ("Blood of Christ") Mountains, these are the tallest dunes in North America. The scale is striking: The dunes contain nearly five billion cubic meters of sand. The best way to get a feel for this ever-changing landscape is to lace up your hiking boots and work your way up to the summit of High Dune—the view from the top gazing across the sandy dunes is sublime.

(Right) Masterworks of wind, water, and earth, the **Great Sand Dunes** reach heights of up to 750 feet.

Great Sand Dunes National Park and Preserve

PLACES TO VISIT IN COLORADO
- Garden of the Gods (Colorado Springs)
- Black Canyon of the Gunnison National Park (Montrose)
- Great Stupa of Dharmakaya (Shambhala Mountain Center, Red Feather Lakes)
- Colorado National Monument (Fruita)
- Glenwood Springs Hot Pool (Glenwood Springs)

WYOMING

YELLOWSTONE NATIONAL PARK

Yellowstone National Park in Wyoming, Montana, and Idaho was the world's first national park. At 2.2 million acres, it is one of North America's largest areas of protected wilderness. These distinctions have preserved Yellowstone's wild nature and made it a model for other parks.

Yellowstone is home to more than half of the world's thermal features, including dramatic geysers such as Old Faithful, steaming fumaroles, bubbling hot pools, and belching mud pots. Yellowstone is one of only two intact geyser basins on the planet.

The Lamar Valley, in Yellowstone's northeastern corner, is known as "The Serengeti of North America." There are more large mammals here—such as deer, moose, elk, bison, bears, and wolves—than in any other ecosystem on the continent.

Yellowstone is also a trove of aquatic wonders, especially Yellowstone Lake (the largest high-altitude lake in the continental United States, at 7,733 feet above sea level) and the spectacular geothermal theatrics on its shores at West Thumb.

(Top right) **The Grand Canyon of the Yellowstone River** is a geological masterwork punctuated by two dramatic waterfalls, 109-foot Upper Falls and 308-foot Lower Falls.

(Bottom right) No trip to Yellowstone is complete without a visit to **Old Faithful**. The geyser erupts every 35 to 120 minutes.

The lakeside thermal features at **West Thumb** are among the many spectacular sights in Yellowstone National Park.

WYOMING PLACES TO VISIT

- National Elk Refuge (Jackson)
- Hot Springs State Park (Thermopolis)
- Bridger-Teton National Forest (Western Wyoming)
- Fort Laramie National Historic Site (Southeast Wyoming)
- Cheyenne Frontier Days (Cheyenne)
- Fossil Butte National Monument (Kemmerer)
- Snowy Range Scenic Byway (Centennial)

The Cathedral Group of the Grand Tetons looms above Jackson Hole, Wyoming, in Grand Teton National Park.

GRAND TETON NATIONAL PARK

The beauty of the Teton Range in northwestern Wyoming is rapturous. Grand Teton National Park is situated in Jackson Hole, the famed valley bounded by Yellowstone to the north and the Tetons to the west. Grand Teton, Mount Owen, and Teewinot are collectively known as the Cathedral Group, and the view of these mountains from the northeast is astounding.

DEVILS TOWER NATIONAL MONUMENT

The origins of the igneous spire known as Devils Tower date back 60 million years, when columns of molten magma cooled a full mile-and-a-half below Earth's crust. After eons of erosion, the soft sedimentary layers that once covered the spire disappeared, and the tower now reaches 867 feet from its base into the sky in northeast Wyoming. Wildlife is abundant in the area. More than 100 species of birds circle in the sky; chipmunks scurry on the tower; and the forested base is alive with rabbits, deer, and porcupines.

(Left) The pillar of igneous rock that is now **Devils Tower** was buried until wind and water swept away the layers of sedimentary rock millions of years ago, revealing the columnar tower.

CODY

Named for its founder, William "Buffalo Bill" Cody, this is one town in the country where the West lives on. Cody, Wyoming, is a bit of a bug in amber, with wooden boardwalks fronting its historic storefronts on the city's main drag. The culture here still smacks of the Old West in many ways. The city bills itself as the "Rodeo Capital of the World." It's the only city in the country that has a nightly rodeo all summer long: the Cody Nite Rodeo.

Outdoor recreation is also big in these parts. The Shoshone River runs right through Cody, and there are mountainous destinations in its backyard, including Yellowstone National Park just 52 miles to the west.

(Right) **The Buffalo Bill Center of the West** is a complex of five museums (dedicated to Native Americans, natural history, Western art, firearms, and "Buffalo Bill" Cody himself) and a research library in Cody.

Medicine Wheel in northern Wyoming has been an active religious site for thousands of years.

MEDICINE WHEEL NATIONAL HISTORIC LANDMARK

Wyoming's Medicine Wheel is in a remote area of the Bighorn National Forest. It is one of the oldest active religious sites on the planet: For 7,000 years, this spot on Medicine Mountain has been sacred. Medicine Wheel is part of a larger system of interrelated religious areas, altars, sweat lodge sites, and other ceremonial venues, and it is still in use. The lasting artifact at the site is the actual Medicine Wheel, which is 75 feet in diameter and composed of 28 "spokes" of rocks intersecting in a central rocky cairn. Medicine Wheel is a National Historic Landmark enclosed by a simple rope fence. It is considered one of the best-preserved sites of its kind.

UTAH

ARCHES NATIONAL PARK

Chiseled by the powerful, perpetual forces of wind and water, this surprising natural rock garden contains the planet's most remarkable collection of abstract sculpture. Arches National Park sits on a great plateau in southeastern Utah, encompassing a stark landscape of broken red sandstone. The park contains more than 2,000 natural stone arches. But these spectacular sandstone portals, braced against the desert sky and revealing lovely desert terrain through their openings, are only part of the stunning landscape here.

Arches National Park's most photographed attraction, **Delicate Arch**, is a famous icon seen on Utah's license plates.

GREAT SALT LAKE

Utah's Great Salt Lake covers about 1,700 square miles in the shadows of the grand Wasatch Range. The lake is a remnant of a prehistoric inland sea called Lake Bonneville that was once ten times bigger than the Great Salt Lake. Visitors enjoy boating and swimming in its waters and sunbathing on white sand beaches. There are also trails for hiking and mountain biking on Antelope Island, a Utah State Park, as well as other stretches of shoreline.

The remnant of a once-vast inland sea, the **Great Salt Lake** has a higher salinity than the Pacific Ocean.

The stunning spires of the **Salt Lake Temple** are the result of four decades of labor.

TEMPLE SQUARE

Temple Square in Salt Lake City is Utah's most visited site. Salt Lake Temple is at its center. This architectural wonder is a living legacy to 40 years of hard work and perseverance. Work on the Salt Lake Temple began in 1853, six years after Brigham Young led thousands of Mormons to the Great Salt Lake to escape persecution in Nauvoo, Illinois. During the next four decades, workers painstakingly carved granite blocks to create the temple. Each block was transported by ox-drawn wagon or railroad to the construction site. Master stonecutters then fit the blocks perfectly into place, without the aid of mortar.

BRYCE CANYON NATIONAL PARK

Bryce Canyon is a spectacular display of geological formations in southern Utah. It is the sculpted side of the Paunsaugunt Plateau that is now a fantasyland covered by thousands of red and orange hoodoos (rock columns). These sandstone towers were left behind when layers of the surrounding rock eroded.

The seeds for Bryce Canyon's dense forest of hoodoos were planted 60 million years ago, when inland seas and lakes covered southwestern Utah. Over eons, sediment collected on the lake's floor and congealed into rock. Later, movements in the earth's crust pushed the Paunsaugunt Plateau skyward, leaving its eastern edge exposed to the ravages of wind and water. The resulting multihued hoodoos are awe-inspiring.

An intricately carved collection of vibrantly colored hoodoos populates the unforgettable landscape of **Bryce Canyon National Park.**

MONUMENT VALLEY

Mythic-looking monoliths of red sandstone loom over the sandy desert floor of Monument Valley in Utah and Arizona. This Navajo Nation Tribal Park offers some of the most enduring images in the West. The formations in Monument Valley were pushed through Earth's surface by geological upheaval and then carved by wind and rivers. Among the most recognizable formations in Monument Valley are the 300-foot-tall, precariously narrow Totem Pole; the arch known as Ear of the Wind; and the East Mitten and West Mitten buttes.

(Right) The rock at **Monument Valley** is stratified in three principal layers, with siltstone atop sandstone atop shale.

ZION NATIONAL PARK

The sheer, vibrantly colored cliff and canyon landscape of Zion stretches across 229 square miles in southwestern Utah. Nine distinct layers of rock can be found throughout the park. The colors of the rocks are accented by traces of iron, creating an array of reds, pinks, whites, and yellows, as well as flashes of black, green, and purple. More than 200 million years ago, the land here was a sea basin, but tectonic forces thrust the land up, and rivers and wind carved the winding canyons.

(Right) The entrance to **Zion National Park** is a gateway to some of the most visually stunning geological formations on the planet.

PLACES TO VISIT IN UTAH

- Capitol Reef National Park (Torrey)
- Lake Powell (Southern Utah)
- Cedar Breaks National Monument (Brian Head)
- Golden Spike National Historic Site (Brigham City)
- Natural Bridges National Monument (Southeast Utah)
- Sundance Film Festival (Park City)
- Dead Horse Point State Park (Moab)

CANYONLANDS NATIONAL PARK

The wide-open wilderness of sandstone canyons in southeast Utah's Canyonlands National Park is the remarkable product of millions of years of rushing water. The Colorado and the Green rivers have shaped this landscape of precipitous chasms and vividly painted mesas, pinnacles, and buttes. The rivers meet and merge at the amazing Confluence in the heart of Canyonlands, dividing the park into four distinct sections: Island in the Sky, a mesa that rises more than 1,000 feet above the rivers; the Needles, a landscape of grassy valleys dominated by banded pinnacles; the Maze, so named for its labyrinth of canyons; and Horseshoe Canyon, known for its rock art and spring wildflowers.

IDAHO

HELLS CANYON OF THE SNAKE RIVER

A huge lake once covered the area now bisected by the Oregon–Idaho state line. The rocky bulge of the Owyhee Mountains kept the Snake and Columbia rivers separate until giving way roughly a million years ago. Then the Snake rapidly cut its way through as much as ten miles of igneous rock to join with the Columbia, chiseling out the chasm now known as the Hells Canyon of the Snake River.

Today, Hells Canyon is one of the continent's most dramatic landscapes. The adjacent mountain ridges rise an average of more than a mile above the canyon floor, towering over the whitewater below. The pinnacle of He Devil Mountain is almost 8,000 feet higher than the river, making for the deepest gorge in the United States.

PLACES TO VISIT IN IDAHO
- Sawtooth National Recreation Area (Central Idaho)
- Boise River Greenbelt (Boise)
- Old Idaho State Penitentiary (Boise)
- Idaho Botanical Garden (Boise)
- Bear Lake (Utah-Idaho border)
- Hells Gate State Park (Lewiston)
- Harriman State Park (Island Park)

Hells Canyon is North America's deepest river gorge.

CRATERS OF THE MOON NATIONAL MONUMENT AND PRESERVE

Called by an early visitor the strangest 75 square miles on the North American continent, Craters of the Moon National Monument and Preserve in south-central Idaho is a remarkable volcanic landscape pockmarked with cinder cones, lava tubes, deep fissures, and lava fields. Rather than one large volcano cone, there are many small craters and fissures through which lava flowed at one time. In some places, the molten lava encased standing trees and then hardened. Eventually, the wood rotted, resulting in bizarre tree-shape lava molds. The landscape is so strange and lunarlike that American astronauts have actually trained at the site.

City of Rocks National Reserve in southern Idaho is famous for its granite outcroppings and popular with rock climbers, hikers, campers, hunters, birders, and photographers.

Visitors to **Lake Coeur d'Alene** in northern Idaho can enjoy hiking, cycling, boating, sailing, fishing, and watching bald eagles feed on kokanee salmon in the lake.

The 212-foot-tall **Shoshone Falls** is also known as the "Niagara of the West." Shoshone Falls is a few miles northeast of Twin Falls, Idaho, in the Snake River Canyon.

The otherworldly landscape at **Craters of the Moon** is a result of a violent volcanic epoch that lasted from 15,000 years ago to 2,000 years ago.

MONTANA

GLACIER NATIONAL PARK

The perfect geometry scoring the sides of the canyons, valleys, cirques, and mountains of Montana's Glacier National Park is the majestic work of nearly extinct glaciers. During the past 60 million years, these glaciers have melted, contracted, receded, and shaped vast areas of rock and earth in northern Montana.

Viewed from the plains east of Glacier National Park, the Rocky Mountains are stunning. They abruptly rise from 4,000 feet in elevation to over 10,000 atop the highest peaks, then just as precipitously drop off to about 3,000 feet at Lake McDonald in the park's southwestern quarter. One thousand miles of rivers and streams and 653 lakes are shoehorned into roughly 1,600 square miles. The trail system covering the rugged terrain is a hiker's paradise.

MUSEUM OF THE ROCKIES

Long before grizzlies and bighorn sheep roamed the Rockies, Montana's claim to fame was wildlife of a different kind—dinosaurs. About 60 million years ago, the region was tropical. Local dinosaurs included the *Tyrannosaurus rex*, *Apatosaurus*, and *Triceratops*, all of which thrived until a climate shift wiped them out. This rich pre-history is told at Bozeman's Museum of the Rockies, home to the largest collection of American dinosaur bones in the world, nearly all of which were discovered in Montana.

(Above) The exhibits at the **Museum of the Rockies** in Bozeman, Montana, dig into dinosaur biology and behavior, as well as fossil recovery and paleontology.

(Left) **Glacier National Park**, named for the rivers of ice that sculpted its dramatic alpine landscape, is the national park many people say they would most like to revisit.

The bleak but beautiful badlands of **Makoshika State Park** in Glendive, Montana, sit in stark contrast to the surrounding plains.

PLACES TO VISIT IN MONTANA

- C.M. Russell Museum (Great Falls)
- Giant Springs State Park (Great Falls)
- Lewis and Clark National Historic Trail Interpretive Center (Great Falls)
- Bighorn Canyon National Recreation Area (Fort Smith)
- Grizzly and Wolf Discovery Center (West Yellowstone)
- Moss Mansion Historic House Museum (Billings)
- World Museum of Mining (Butte)
- Big Hole National Battlefield (Wisdom)
- Flathead Lake (near Kalispell)

The memorial on **Last Stand Hill** was built over the mass grave of 7th Cavalry soldiers, U.S. Indian scouts, and others who died here.

LITTLE BIGHORN BATTLEFIELD NATIONAL MONUMENT

The Little Bighorn Battlefield National Monument memorializes the site where on June 25–26, 1876, Lieutenant Colonel George Custer and the U.S. Army's 7th Cavalry were defeated by a far larger Lakota and Cheyenne war party during what became known as Custer's Last Stand. Custer and more than 200 soldiers under his command perished in the battle, as did at least 60 Cheyenne and Lakota. Despite the outcome, Custer's Last Stand marked the end for the Cheyenne and Lakota people's nomadic way of life in the West.

CALIFORNIA

REDWOOD NATIONAL AND STATE PARKS

Near remote stretches of northwest California's oceanfront, the water, soil, and sun blend perfectly for redwood growth. The results are the astounding redwood forests. More than 100,000 acres of soul-stirring forest are protected under the auspices of Redwood National and State Parks, the last spot in North America where the trees thrive in size and number.

The tallest redwood in the parks is more than twice as tall as the Statue of Liberty. The parks' tallest trees, located in the aptly named Tall Trees Grove, measure about 360 feet from base to treetop, heights that have taken them more than 600 years to attain.

NAPA VALLEY VINEYARDS

Napa Valley is only five miles across at its widest point and 30 miles long, but its reputation stretches around the world. About 50 miles north of San Francisco, the valley is home to roughly 100,000 people, five incorporated cities, and at least 300 wineries. The long-standing success of the local wine industry is a result of the climate and soil, which are ideal for growing grapes. The soil is especially diverse: fully half of the varieties of soil on the planet are found within the confines of Napa Valley.

(Above) **The Napa Valley** was carved by the Napa River, which flows directly into the San Francisco Bay and attracts anglers and paddlers. But most visitors come for the fresh air, the good food, and, of course, the great wine.

(Left) **The coast redwood**, *Sequoia sempervirens*, is the tallest known plant species in the world.

CHINATOWN

San Francisco's Chinatown is the largest Chinatown on the continent, and it explodes with color every day of the year. Chinatown is one of the Bay Area's most visited tourist hotspots, with plenty of eateries, bars, and shops. But it also serves as an authentic neighborhood where people live, work, and play. If you're in San Francisco around the beginning of the year, you might be lucky enough to see the Chinese New Year Parade (a San Francisco tradition since just after the 1849 Gold Rush).

The Chinese New Year Parade is now the biggest illuminated nighttime parade in North America.

The landmark granite formation **Half Dome** was once considered impossible to climb.

YOSEMITE VALLEY

The unmistakable panorama of Yosemite Valley in central California reveals a dazzling wonderland of granite sculpted over eons by ice, wind, and water. Waterfalls cascade down the granite cliffs, the most famous of which is Yosemite Falls, at 2,425 feet the tallest waterfall in North America. Yosemite Valley is bookended by two famous geologic masterworks. These hulking, distinct formations are known worldwide: Half Dome rises 4,800 feet above the eastern end of the valley, while the 3,600-foot El Capitán (Spanish for "the captain") stands sentry at the western entrance, fronted by one of the sheerest cliffs in the world.

(Left) In 1884, Sarah Winchester, heiress to the Winchester Rifle Company, visited a fortune-teller after the death of her husband and baby daughter. The medium told her that her fate was tied to her house: Continuous building would appease the evil spirits and help her attain eternal life. Winchester continued building her San José, California, mansion for the ensuing 38 years, spending the bulk of her multimillion-dollar inheritance in the process. Today, visitors can tour the **Winchester Mystery House**. The house is designated a California historical landmark and is listed on the National Register of Historic Places.

GOLDEN GATE BRIDGE

San Francisco's Golden Gate Bridge does for the West Coast what the Statue of Liberty and the Manhattan skyline do for the East: It welcomes newcomers while proclaiming the golden, youthful promise of the new world. The bridge was named not for its color (it's actually orange vermilion) but because it spans the Golden Gate Strait, named by explorer John C. Fremont. The beautiful bridge is also the centerpiece of the Golden Gate National Recreation Area. Golden Gate is the most popular destination in the national parks system, with more than 14 million visitors each year.

(Right) At 4,200 feet from tower to tower, **Golden Gate Bridge** reigned as the world's longest suspension bridge for 27 years.

ALCATRAZ ISLAND

Kids will love their visit to the country's most noted lockup, where audio tours discuss some of the various escape attempts that have become a part of the island's history. The boat trip to Alcatraz Island is just part of the entertainment. You'll find tour boats docked between Fisherman's Wharf and Pier 39. This area offers a hodgepodge of tourist delights, and youngsters will love browsing the souvenir shops and watching the street performers while you wait for your boat.

(Above) You'll be treated to breathtaking views of the San Francisco skyline and the Golden Gate Bridge as you travel across the bay to **Alcatraz Island**.

(Below) A brutally beautiful land of extremes, **Death Valley National Park** is found near the California-Nevada border, northwest of Las Vegas. The temperature there has reached 134 degrees Fahrenheit, while average annual rainfall is less than two inches—this makes Death Valley the driest spot on the continent.

Casa Grande's more than 100 rooms are the setting for Hearst's priceless collection of European art and antiques.

HEARST CASTLE

Over the course of nearly three decades, newspaper baron William Randolph Hearst built this luxurious and legendary home on the 250,000-acre San Simeon, California, ranch he inherited in 1919. An opulent example of Mediterranean Revival architecture, the estate's prime attraction is Casa Grande, the 60,645-square-foot main house.

LA BREA TAR PITS

Rancho La Brea is in the heart of urban Los Angeles, so it's hard to imagine that millions of years ago it was submerged in the ocean, teeming with sea life. When the Pacific Ocean receded about 100,000 years ago, sediments sheathed the area and fossil fuels formed below the surface.

About 40,000 years ago, oil began to seep through the labyrinth of fissures and permeable rock, creating what are now known as the La Brea Tar Pits. Back then, dire wolves, sabertooth tigers, mastodons, mammoths, and giant sloths roamed the area. The oily tar pits captured and trapped many animals one by one. These animals' unfortunate fate translates into an exceptional fossil record preserved in the pits.

Archaeologists have unearthed an entire prehistoric ecosystem at the **La Brea Tar Pits**, from plants and insects to camels and bison.

PLACES TO VISIT IN CALIFORNIA
- Disneyland (Anaheim)
- Exploratorium: The Museum of Science, Art, and Human Perception (San Francisco)
- Point Reyes National Seashore (south of San Francisco)
- San Diego Zoo (San Diego)
- San Diego Zoo Safari Park (Escondido)
- SeaWorld (San Diego)
- Santa Catalina Island (near Los Angeles)

The Hollywood sign was put up in 1923.

HOLLYWOOD

The rolling Hollywood Hills, clad in a lush layer of greenery, cradle neighborhoods of all kinds and feature a one-of-a-kind American icon, the Hollywood sign. Down below, on Hollywood Boulevard, the side-walk sports 2,600 terrazzo-and-brass stars that immortalize giants of the entertainment industry. The street is a colorful spot for people-watching and is the address of Mann's Chinese Theatre, perhaps the most famous cinema in the world.

SEQUOIA AND KINGS CANYON NATIONAL PARKS

General Sherman is the leader among trees. This huge sequoia tops off at 275 feet—as tall as a 26-story building. It is Sequoia's most famous resident and is one of the largest living organisms in the world—its diameter is a gargantuan 36 feet. Thousands of General Sherman's relatives fill the pristine forests of these two spectacular national parks, which are in central California, east of Fresno.

Before this tree at **Sequoia National Park** fell in 1937, it stood 275 feet high. Rather than attempt its removal, the park service carved a tunnel through it that measures 17 feet wide and 8 feet high.

MONTEREY BAY AQUARIUM

Monterey Bay Aquarium is located in the converted former Hovden Cannery, which canned squid and sardines until the early 1970s on Monterey's legendary Cannery Row. The aquarium is home to more than 30,000 aquatic creatures, with everything from jellyfish to sharks. The exhibits are fed by water that comes directly from Monterey Bay, which hosts one of the most diverse marine ecosystems on the planet. The mudflats, kelp forests, and nutrient-rich water support all sorts of sea life in the confines of the bay.

Hiking trails follow the **Big Sur coastline**, where you'll probably catch a glimpse of sea otters floating on their backs and snacking on abalone.

BIG SUR COASTLINE

This scenic stretch of coastline has a breathtaking beauty that invites many stops for pictures. One minute you're standing atop a high cliff looking down at a crashing sapphire sea, and the next you're hiking through a misty redwood forest. The Big Sur coastline begins just south of Monterey, California, where Point Lobos Reserve encompasses a group of headlands, coves, and rolling meadows. Between the months of December and May, migrating gray whales are a common sight.

One of the finest aquariums in the United States—and quite possibly the world—the **Monterey Bay Aquarium** attracts almost two million visitors a year.

OREGON

PIONEER COURTHOUSE SQUARE

Pioneer Courthouse Square attracts millions of visitors each year, many coming to see the two amphitheaters that host more than 300 happenings every year, including concerts and cultural festivals; the annual midsummer Festival of Flowers; the fountain; pillars; sculptures; and the astounding Weather Machine, an innovative creation with three symbols that each represent an element of Portland's climate.

Pioneer Courthouse Square is nicknamed "Portland's Living Room." And like every good living room, the square offers entertainment and plenty of seating space.

CRATER LAKE NATIONAL PARK

The intense blue of Crater Lake is striking. The vivid color is due in part to the depth of this freshwater lake. At its deepest, the lake's floor plunges 1,932 feet below the surface, making it the deepest lake in the United States.

This lake in southwest Oregon was created centuries ago when rain and snowmelt filled a caldera, a huge bowl that was the remnant of a volcano. During some years, the lake is replenished by wintertime snowfalls of 50 feet or more. Because no water flows through the lake, it remains pure and tranquil.

Green algae grows at a record depth of 725 feet below the surface, indicating that sunlight may penetrate deeper into **Crater Lake** than any other body of water in the world.

MOUNT HOOD

Picture-perfect Mount Hood is a visual reminder to city dwellers in Portland that the great outdoors is just a short drive away—only 47 miles east. At 11,239 feet above sea level, the peak is the fourth-highest in the Cascade Range. Like all of its Cascade brethren, Mount Hood is a volcano, and an active one. It erupted twice in the mid-1800s and has had at least four eruptive periods in the past 15,000 years. The volcanic cone atop the mountain is dominated by snow and ice, with glaciers and snowfields shrouding it year-round.

Mount Hood is a recreational paradise, with popular ski resorts, hiking routes, and backcountry trails.

Located at the summit of the volcano almost 8,000 feet above sea level, the nearly 20-square-mile **Newberry Caldera** has two idyllic alpine lakes, one of which drains into a magnificent waterfall.

NEWBERRY NATIONAL VOLCANIC MONUMENT

In the heart of central Oregon's Deschutes National Forest, Newberry National Volcanic Monument sits atop an active geothermal hotspot. The crux of this hotspot is the huge Newberry Volcano. When Newberry last erupted about 1,300 years ago it created a devastatingly beautiful caldera. The volcano's flanks of hardened lava are dotted by hundreds of cinder cones and fissure vents. Today, the once-red-hot landscape can be explored via the Trail of the Molten Land.

MORE OREGON PLACES TO VISIT

- Abert Rim (Lake County)
- Astoria (Pacific Coast)
- Fort Clatsop National Memorial (Astoria)
- Osprey Observation Point (Cascade Lakes Scenic Byway)
- Sea Lion Caves (Lane County)
- Wallowa Lake (Northeast Oregon)
- Vista House (Columbia River Gorge)

Many visitors take the foot trail up to **Benson Bridge** for one of the best spots to view the falls. Look up to see the thin ribbon of the upper falls, or peer down to see the powerful lower cascade as it empties into the Columbia River.

MULTNOMAH FALLS

Ancient Multnomah Falls is a sight to behold. Cascading from its origin on Larch Mountain, it highlights the picturesque Columbia River Gorge in central Oregon. At 620 feet, it's the second-tallest year-round waterfall in the nation. The falls are fed by an underground spring that provides a continuous flow of crystal-clear water that's enhanced by seasonal snowmelt and spring rainstorms.

PIKE PLACE MARKET

Pike Place Market is one of Seattle's most famous landmarks and tourist attractions. More than 100 farmers and 200 artists and craftspeople occupy the market's three levels, which offer the best of Washington's seasonal flowers and produce. Visitors can shop among the vivid colors of exquisite tulips and daffodils in early spring and enjoy juicy golden Rainier cherries in early summer, blueberries in August, and all kinds of high-quality, locally grown produce year-round.

The fishmongers at **Pike Place Market** put on one of the best shows in town. They toss the catch of the day through the air like footballs as they engage the customers in all kinds of banter.

WASHINGTON

SPACE NEEDLE

Seattle's Space Needle is the most popular tourist attraction in the city, receiving more than a million visitors each year. Originally built for the 1962 World's Fair and still the defining feature on the Emerald City's skyline, the 605-foot Space Needle was the tallest building west of the Mississippi when it was completed in late 1961. The futuristic blueprints for the Space Needle evolved from artist Edward E. Carlson's visionary doodle on a placemat. His collaboration with architect John Graham resulted in a prototype space age design that looks a bit like a flying saucer balanced on three giant supports.

The Space Needle was built to withstand winds of up to 200 miles per hour. Wind does cause the needle to sway, but the top house has only closed once—for an hour-and-a-half in 1993 due to 90-mile-per-hour winds.

OLYMPIC NATIONAL PARK

Olympic National Park, in northwestern Washington, is home to one of the most lush, impenetrable rainforests on the planet. Some areas in the park get up to 167 inches of rain a year—more than any other spot in the continental United States. But the beauty of Olympic National Park doesn't end with the rainforest. It is one of the most diverse national parks in the United States. The untouched Pacific coastline is ruggedly beautiful, and the majestic Olympic Mountains rise from the heart of the peninsula. Although the western side of the park is deluged by rain, the eastern side is just the opposite—it's one of the most parched spots on the West Coast north of Los Angeles.

Whale watching is a popular pastime, particularly around Friday Harbor on **San Juan Island**. Take a whale-watching boat tour or head to Lime Kiln Point State Park to play in the sand and watch orcas feed just 30 feet from shore.

SAN JUAN ISLANDS

North of Seattle in Puget Sound sits the San Juan Archipelago, a collection of 172 named islands and another several hundred rocky island outcroppings that appear at low tide. Although about 40 of these idyllic islands are inhabited, most people living here reside on the four that have ferry service: San Juan, Orcas, Lopez, and Shaw. The islands' sheltered waters are home to harbor seals, sea lions, sea otters, dolphins, and orcas.

The rain supports a landscape covered by moss, lichen, and fern, giving the forest at **Olympic National Park** a vibrant green glow.

MUSEUM OF GLASS

The Museum of Glass is Tacoma, Washington's splashy contribution to the contemporary art world. Its works in different media have one thing in common: They all incorporate glass. Visitors can browse permanent and temporary exhibitions of all kinds of contemporary glass art. The museum's Visiting Artist Collection is permanent, featuring works created on-site in the Hot Shop Amphitheater. The Hot Shop has hot and cold glass studios and seating for 138 visitors.

The Chihuly Bridge of Glass connects the museum to downtown Tacoma. The 500-foot steel-and-glass pedestrian bridge is adorned with colorful glass spires.

Come summertime, **Mount Rainier**'s subalpine meadows explode with color as lupines, monkeyflowers, asters, and myriad other species bloom. The kaleidoscope of multihued flora is a startling contrast to the stark blue and white of the looming peak.

MOUNT RAINIER NATIONAL PARK

The world of snow and ice atop Mount Rainier, 14,410 feet above sea level and 70 miles from Seattle, never thaws. At times, the annual snowfall exceeds 90 feet on the mountain's slopes. But below Mount Rainier's frosty covering, conditions are the polar opposite: Inside, the mountain is an active volcano, and it's the tallest one in the volcanic Cascade Range.

MORE WASHINGTON PLACES TO VISIT

- Cape Flattery Light (Strait of Juan de Fuca)
- Klondike Gold Rush Museum (Seattle)
- Manito Park (Spokane)
- Mount Saint Helens (100 miles from Seattle)
- Puget Sound (northwestern coast)
- Snoqualmie Valley Historical Museum (North Bend)
- Spokane Falls (Spokane)

ALASKA

DENALI NATIONAL PARK AND PRESERVE

Denali means "The High One" in the native Athabascan tongue. It's an apt moniker, considering that the 20,320-foot-tall mountain—also known as Mount McKinley—is North America's highest peak. It's also one of the most striking mountains in the world—when it's visible from the surrounding subarctic plateau. Because the park is so far north—240 miles north of Anchorage, Alaska—its mountains are not forested like the Rockies and the Sierra Nevada. At Denali's northern latitude, the timberline falls between 2,000 and 3,000 feet. Below the rugged high country are tundra-covered lowlands. Immense glaciers connect the two, creeping down Denali and the neighboring peaks.

(Above) Denali has earned the nickname "The Subarctic Serengeti" for its thriving wildlife population. Denali's "big five" mammals are grizzly bears, gray wolves, caribou, Dall's sheep, and moose.

(Below) The park that encompasses Denali and the adjacent mountains of the Alaska Range is a vast, pristine wilderness larger than the state of Massachusetts.

GLACIER BAY NATIONAL PARK AND PRESERVE

Glacier Bay is Alaska's southernmost national park. It is also a living laboratory where scientists study glacial recession. The ice in and around Glacier Bay is melting at a remarkable pace; in fact, the phenomenon is the fastest glacial retreat on record. When Captain George Vancouver first charted these waters in 1794, what is now the bay was little more than an indention in a vast sheet of ice that extended for hundreds of miles. During the next 200 years, the glaciers receded more than 60 miles, creating a masterpiece of rock, ice, and water.

(Above) Massive glaciers and majestic mountains, some of which have peaks 15,000 feet above sea level, ring Glacier Bay.

(Below) Glacier Bay is also a critical wildlife habitat, sustaining humpback whales, orcas, porpoises, seals, and sea otters in its waters and moose, black bears, brown bears, wolves, and deer on the shore.

Each totem pole at Saxman Native Village is unique. The colorful carvings share the stories of their makers and the stories of the villages where they once stood.

SAXMAN NATIVE VILLAGE

This is the world's largest totem park, consisting of two dozen ornate totem poles in Saxman, near Ketchikan in southeast Alaska. Most of the poles are not dated and were reclaimed from abandoned Tlingit villages in the 1930s by the Civilian Conservation Corps and the United States Forest Service.

FIVE FINGER LIGHT

The fabled inside passage of the Alaskan panhandle has been a favorite of maritime travelers since the days of John Muir. The distinguished naturalist wrote regularly of the scenic wonders of the coastal region for *Century* magazine in the late 19th century. Even at that time, the area was known for its dangerous shoals and reefs. For that reason, a lighthouse was placed on an island just north of Kupreanof Island in 1902. The area was known as "the five fingers" by shippers for the fingerlike shape of the forested islands.

The current lighthouse, with its art deco style, was completed in 1935, after the original wooden keeper's home and lighthouse burned down. Built of reinforced concrete, the new main building also serves as a sturdy platform for the nearly 70-foot tower.

Located about 70 miles south of Alaska's state capital, Juneau, the **Five Finger Light** is often seen by those who take the Alaska Maritime Highway on scenic summer cruise vessels.

GATES OF THE ARCTIC NATIONAL PARK AND PRESERVE

America's northernmost national park, Gates of the Arctic National Park and Preserve, has to be the most remote by any measure. It has no roads and no trails in from the outside. The entirety of Gates of the Arctic lies north of the Arctic Circle. The park is the centerpiece of 700 square miles of protected range, with the Noatak Preserve to the west and the Arctic National Wildlife Refuge to the east.

Things to do at the park and preserve include float plane trips, camping, hiking, rock climbing, bird-watching, and backpacking. Popular sites to visit include Anaktuvuk Pass, Frigid Crags, Boreal Mountain, Mount Doonarak, Arrigetch Peaks, and Mount Igikpak.

It is a paradox of the **Gates of the Arctic National Park and Preserve** that this is one of the few national parks to contain communities. People have lived in what is now part of the park for about 12,500 years. Nearly all of the Nunamiut people are mountain Inuit who traditionally traveled between the Brooks Range and the Arctic coast, feeding on migrating herds of caribou.

ALASKA PLACES TO VISIT
- AJ Mine/Gastineau Mill (Juneau)
- Alaska Aviation Heritage Museum (Anchorage)
- Iditarod Trail Sled Dog Race (Anchorage)
- Katmai National Park (Southern Alaska)
- Kenai Fjords National Park (near Seward)
- Lake Clark National Park (Southern Alaska)
- Kobuk Valley National Park (Northwestern Alaska)
- Wrangell-St. Elias National Park (Southeastern Alaska)

HAWAII

MAUNA LOA

Part of Hawaiian Volcanoes National Park, Mauna Loa (meaning "Long Mountain") rises 13,677 feet above the blue surface of the Pacific Ocean. Although many mountain peaks rise higher than Mauna Loa, its actual size is nothing short of astonishing. Measured from its base, which is 18,000 feet underwater, Mauna Loa exceeds even Mount Everest in height—by a full 2,000 feet. Atop the summit of Mauna Loa, a caldera called Mokuaweoweo features a number of craters that have previously erupted. The caldera floor is covered with lava contorted into otherworldly formations, daunting pits, and towering cinder cones.

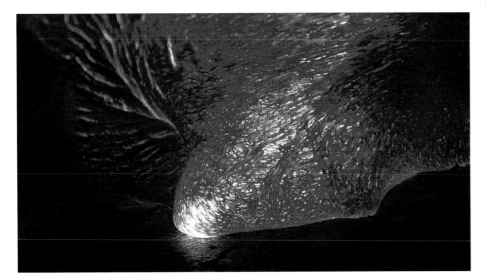

Current-day eruptions within the crater of **Mauna Loa** are relatively harmless. Volcanologists have been able to reliably predict activity. Because of this, an impending eruption typically draws thousands of people to the crater's rim.

HALEAKALA NATIONAL PARK

Haleakala is actually an enormous volcano that—although dormant since 1790—is a striking reminder of the power seething below Earth's surface. Impressive cinder cones and lava sculptures on the upper slopes of Haleakala are lasting remnants of furious, tumultuous moments in its past. At the base of Haleakala, the lush, green Kipahulu Valley unravels to the coast. This tropical ecosystem is a distant memory from the volcano's 10,000-foot summit: Guava trees and ferns below give way to yellow brush known as mamane and the silversword plant, unique to the volcano.

As legend has it, a long time ago the god Maui captured the sun in a great mountain's summit basin on a Hawaiian island. The mountain came to be known as **Haleakala**, Hawaiian for "House of the Sun."

HANAKAPI'AI FALLS

Named for a Hawaiian princess, Hanakapi'ai Falls on the northwestern side of the island of Kauai is the picture of tropical paradise. The falls are a popular destination for experienced hikers. The four-mile Kalalua Trail, which leads to the falls, begins at Ke'e Beach. From Ke'e Beach, follow the trail upslope to the Hanakapi'ai Valley, a lush cradle of greenery dotted with a vibrant array of wildflowers. From there the trail continues down to the secluded Hanakapi'ai Beach and the start of the final two-mile leg to Hanakapi'ai Falls. Once you reach the falls, you'll be rewarded with breathtaking views and a relaxing swim in its tranquil pools.

At ten miles long, one mile wide, and more than 3,500 feet deep, **Waimea Canyon** on the Hawaiian island of Kauai is the largest canyon in the Pacific.

The beautiful, 300-foot ribbon of water delicately cascades down a rugged volcanic wall, tumbling into an idyllic pool at **Hanakapi'ai Falls**.

WAIMEA CANYON

Dubbed "The Grand Canyon of the Pacific" by Mark Twain, Waimea Canyon's sharply eroded cliffs reveal layers of vivid colors that seem to change in the sun. Unlike the Grand Canyon, plentiful rainfall keeps this canyon and its surrounding area thick with vegetation, and visitors are frequently treated to the sight of vivid rainbows.

HAWAII PLACES TO VISIT
- 'Iolani Palace (Big Island)
- Makapuu Point (Oahu)
- Olowalu Petroglyphs (Maui)
- Pearl Harbor/World War II Valor in the Pacific National Monument (Oahu)
- Polynesian Cultural Center (Oahu)
- Valley of the Temples (Oahu)

Waikiki is an excellent place to learn to surf, and lessons are available at just about every hotel or water sports center on the beach.

WAIKIKI BEACH
This famous two-mile stretch of sand in Oahu is home to scores of family-friendly beach hotels and all kinds of action-packed excitement. Kids will enjoy strolling along the beachfront promenade, stopping for shaved ice or an ice cream cone, taking a dip in the ocean, and checking out the parade of people passing by.